No-one Else Has
Complained

As this is a good place for dedications—
to Dominic and Patty

No-one Else Has Complained

CLEMENT FREUD

Illustrated by
RICHARD WILLSON

ELM TREE BOOKS · LONDON

ELM TREE BOOKS

Published by the Penguin Group
27 Wrights Lane, London W8 5TZ, England
Viking Penguin Inc, 40 West 23rd Street, New York, New York 10010, U.S.A.
Penguin Books Australia Ltd, Ringwood, Victoria, Australia
Penguin Books Canada Ltd, 2801 John Street, Markham, Ontario, Canada L3R 1B4
Penguin Books (N.Z.) Ltd, 182–190 Wairau Road, Auckland 10, New Zealand

Penguin Books Ltd, Registered Offices: Harmondsworth, Middlesex, England

First published in Great Britain 1988 by
Elm Tree Books

Research by Sophie Watson

1 3 5 7 9 10 8 6 4 2

British Library Cataloguing in Publication Data

Freud, Clement
No-one else has complained.
1. Restaurants, lunch rooms, etc.
I. Title
647'.95   TX945

ISBN 0–241–11853–0

Printed in Great Britain by
Richard Clay Ltd, Bungay, Suffolk

Contents

The lines from Hilaire Belloc's *Cautionary Verses* on p. 1 are quoted by permission of Gerald Duckworth.

Foreword

This book is intended to help the customer, not the caterer, for whom customers are the single most disruptive element in the restaurant/hotel trade. An empty establishment is one that has no short-term problems. It is only when guests arrive, all at the same time, and order the same item of food from the *à la carte* menu – or won't eat the cauliflower with their mixed grill – that the aggro begins.

However, over the years, caterers have reluctantly realised that without customers it is jolly hard to pay their butlers and keep up their standard of living . . . they have also realised that the more ill-at-ease and apprehensive the punter, the simpler is it to serve him, the less trouble is he likely to give.

The English middle class, from which the bulk of restaurant clientèle is drawn, is uniquely suited to the villainies of the trade; if caterers had programmed their concept of an ideal customer into a computer, it would have come up with pretty much what exists: someone reared on the maxims of Eat Up, Don't Make A Fuss and Nice People Don't Look At Their Bills. Belloc sums it up well when he writes of Charles Augustus Fortescue

And often at his father's board
He'd ask them of his own accord
To give him – if they didn't mind –
The greasiest morsels they could find.

This book is written to redress the balance, rather as during the war we were given classes called Know the Enemy. It is dedicated to those inhibited by the mystique of restaurants, to them who think that waiters actually speak foreign languages, believe that everyone in a tall white hat is necessarily a genius who knows it all and may pull a knife; that wines called Trockenbeerenauslese should be pronounced so that the waiter can correct the mispronunciation. That there is some good reason – other than to undermine the client's confidence – for a menu to be written in a language not understood by the majority of customers.

NOTE: Customers are referred to in this text as 'he'. Of the two alternatives we came out in favour of the masculine gender not for any sexist reason but because there are marginally more men than women who go to restaurants and writing him/her, he/she does detract from a text. Apologies to women, to whom this book is dedicated every bit as much as it is to men.

A Useful Glossary

Restaurant, café, cafeteria, coffee bar, coffee house, snack bar, brasserie, causerie, buttery, trattoria, bistro.

These words all denote places where refreshments or meals are provided for the public. The most widely used term in the group, and the one with the widest range of meaning, is: *restaurant*. A restaurant can be anything from a small intimate place to a very large establishment with many rooms. Restaurants can serve a variety of food or they can specialise — in French, Italian, Chinese, Indian, etc., cuisine — and are with few exceptions licensed to serve drinks. At some restaurants live music is played, often by a dead-looking pianist or a small combination of instrumentalists. You can usually ask the pianist to play tunes of your choice — or pay him to stop. Restaurants may be open for a relatively short time each day: this depends on the presence of clients and the industry of the proprietor.

Brasserie: There is an expectation on the part of those of us with instinctive feelings about these matters, that brasseries are open for breakfast and do not give you a bread plate.

Buttery: There is some really good definition of buttery which has hardly anything to do with butter. I cannot recall where I saw it — but it seemed meaningful at the time. The dictionary says it is 'a store room for liquor, or provisions generally' which seems useful enough.

Causerie: Claridges have an upmarket self-service restaurant under this name. There may be many more. In French the word means a chat – and there was never much merit in a dry chat on an empty stomach.

Bistro: An Italian restaurant of smallish proportions in which the staff wear open necked shirts and gold medallions on long gold chains. The owner has the most medallions and the fewest buttons done up, and the importance of the rest of the staff is gauged by their decoration in this area. Food in bistros tends to pretentiousness – else they call it a

Trattoria: A bistro in which the staff do not have to wear medallions, but have to kiss the customers as they come in.

Café: At the end of the last century the upper class French thought it a good idea to call their babies by the names of English servants. The same inverted snobbery means that café can refer to anything from a shack with four tables and a lunatic making undrinkable tea to the Café Royal, one of London's most prestigious banqueting locations and once Oscar Wilde's favourite restaurant ... a fact they can no longer advertise because of Clause 28 of the Local Government Act 1988, which prohibits positive promotion of homosexuals.

'A tavern-keeper knows how to get to market and how to feed so many people at a public table. A hotel-keeper is a gentleman who stands on a level with his guests.' (Charles A. Stetson)

The Restaurant Owner: Usually an *haute couturier* who fell out with his backers. Sometimes an accountant who became jealous when he audited the books of a restaurateur and, because his

man was an oaf, the accountant thought he could do just as well. An owner's desire is to have customers who spend enormous amounts of money and depart quickly to make room for others of the same trend. In short he wants an easy life: customers who behave nicely, settle their bills, leave the staff satisfied by paying the service charge and a little bit on top and then say thank you, tell their friends, and come again.

In fact owners spend little time in their own establishments; when it is empty they are out seeing how the competition is doing; when it is full they are out trying to persuade staff from rival restaurants to come and work for them. The situation is now so bad that the average restaurant is filled with other restaurateurs checking the competition or poaching staff, food writers having a free meal and getting material, Enviromental Health Officers on an anonymous tour of inspection (paid for from the rates) and the occasional down-market gossip columnist looking for copy and wondering why there is no room for all the famous people who want to eat there. The business is in a bad way.

The Head Waiter: Is foreign. Just like that. If he is not, he is the exception which proves the rule, for all head waiters are foreign. Speak to him in a foreign language, he will appreciate that; head waiters always like to speak in a foreign language. They especially like the easy words: *Bonjour, monsieur, signora, tagliatelli, benissimo.* The hard words come in English, for instance We Don't Accept Traveller's Cheques/Credit Cards/Portuguese Escudos/Teetotallers.

The head waiter has a decent salary — say £300 a week after tax — and the use of a car. This does not stop the head waiter from trying to grab his share of the tips. Other waiters, who should get the tips, are paid a low hourly wage. The reason for cutting the head waiter in on tips is that he knows who is a good, who a mean customer . . . and if he doesn't get a share from the waiters, he will seat all the mean tippers at the uncooperative waiters' tables.

The Chef: Is interested in making money and doing no more work than is strictly necessary – unless he is employed by an enlightened owner who cuts him in on the overall turnover. If the chef is given a bonus on the profit, that provides him with the incentive to buy cheaply and dish out small portions. Many chefs have been trained for their work, although there is an increasing number of 'natural' chefs. There is also a mounting band of gorillas in white coats who operate the microwave and should by rights be called mechanics.

The Wine Butler: Is the one with the oval medallion around his neck, or occasionally a silver cup dangling from a button-hole to denote his office. Where a wine butler is employed, he is an integral part of the attack. 'Table number 16 is giving trouble,' says the waiter. 'Send in the sommelier,' snaps the manager. Along comes the leather-bound volume of lists of wine, usually starting with champagne so that the *really* scared punter will plunge for the first bottle that catches his eye and the establishment will reap rich rewards. There is something basically hopeless about the function of the knowledgeable wine butler: if people understand wine they don't need his help, if they don't understand, they are not going to learn in the course of a minute's nervous discussion. In a few enlightened liberal restaurants, the wine butler is consulted about, or even chooses, the house wines. Ask the wine butler what has been his input in the selection, and if it was substantial, tell him, 'In that case it would be a great insult if I asked for anything else.' Ask him to soak off the label of the house wine bottle so that you can paste it in your scrap book and treasure it for always. Little things like that please him.

I used to advertise for waiters in the personal column of *Time and Tide, Poultry World* and the *Catholic Herald*, adding that previous experience disqualified applicants. I would sooner be served by someone pleasant and unjaundiced by years of cut and thrust with other establishments' clientèle, than by what is known as a professional waiter, the kind that can balance three smoked salmon plates on his hand, and another four up his arm. Let me warn you about professional waiters. They are there to serve *and to be tipped*. They feel that the greater their input into your meal, the greater will be your realisation that they were essential to your enjoyment. As a result, they will bring you bread in one journey, come back with the butter, go away and fetch the toast, leave your wine ten yards from the table so that you either have to cross the room or need the waiter's help to have a drink . . . and if you do try to help yourself they appear at your elbow to wrestle the wine, water or pepper grinder from your hand. Remember that all this is a game. If they think you know better, they will serve you decently. Ask them with what strength of flour the bread was baked, or whether you can't have unsalted butter. Tell them that you do on the whole prefer sea salt. The golden rule is to *flummox the waiter*, before he is able to get down to flummoxing you.

The History of the Restaurant

There is nothing new about restaurants . . . poor Chaucer's pilgrims who shouted their stories to each other on the road from one pub to another 500 years ago were not being innovative. When someone invented travelling, someone else invented places where travellers could eat and drink – it was as simple as that. Of course there were hiccups – like pregnant women having to be accommodated in the stables because there was no room inside – but over the years things got better.

Restaurant is a French word, literally meaning a restorative.

It was first used in the eighteenth century as a place where the halt and the lame were given a sustaining soup so that they could move on and be halt and lame elsewhere.

The idea of food as a pleasure rather than a necessity has been around for a very long time indeed. Romans had many good ideas long before they had occurred to anyone else (straight roads, chickens) and one of them was the possibility of trying other people's cuisine (the Australians only recently noticed that it is possible to eat things other than kangaroo steaks). The Romans found the English pretty barbaric, but they loved our oysters and went to great lengths to export them to Rome, not that they can have been too good when they arrived. And long before the Romans arrived in Britain, they went to Greece and took Greek chefs back to Rome to teach them how to cook kebabs and houmous. Moving cooks around continued to be a way of cheering up local cuisine for centuries — Italians claim French cooking only really took off after Catherine de Medici arrived in France with Italian cooks. Chitterlings and stuffed goslings were among her imports.

Some smart restaurants now like to discourage casual, or the 'wrong', trade by insisting that male customers wear ties. If they come without one, they can be lent one by the management. The Romans thought that one up, too, and would issue garlands to their guests as they arrived at the feast.

Another idea of the Romans' that caught on was that of inns and inn signs. An ivy bush, or the picture of one, meant that food was available — so The Bush is probably the oldest inn name in Britain. Once the idea of having food and drink for sale caught on, everyone thought it was a good way of making a bit of extra money and the pub signs grew and grew until a law had to be passed in 1419 outlawing any sign that stuck out more than seven feet over the King's highway — too many accidents were caused by passers-by riding into inn signs.

By the middle of the fifteenth century the merchant classes made inn-keeping a popular occupation, and more and more inns began to open. It was not until the Tudor period that an inn would actually offer a private room, and right until the middle of the last century you were likely to have to share. The hero of *Moby Dick* starts his adventures with an indifferent meal and a headshrinker as a bedmate in the Spouter Inn.

But although hostelries have been open for travellers for centuries, it is only recently that people began to go out to eat just for the sake of it. And that was really when the trouble started – weary travellers arriving at a tavern were given whatever was going – no nonsense with menus and decisions – which went on until the nineteenth century. Until then 'pot luck' meant just what it said; which does not mean there was no competition. Harrison's description of England, written in 1583, shows how the owners vied for customers: 'It is a world to see how ech owner of them contendeth with other for goodnesse of interteinement of their ghests, as about finesse and change of linnen, furniture of bedding, beautie of roomes, service at the table, costlinesse of plate, strengthe of drinke, varietie of wines, or well using of horsses.' Amazingly not variation of food.

The fashion grew until, in the early seventeenth century, England could honestly boast of its hotels and the quality of its food (three centuries have passed and the years have taken their toll). In 1625 Fynes Moryson wrote that 'the world affoords not such Innes as England hath, either for good and cheape entertainment after the Guests owne pleasure . . . yea in the very poore Villages, where if Curcilio of Plautus should see the thatched houses, he would fall into a fainting of his spirits, but if he should smell the variety of meates, his starveling look would be much cheared.'

The seventeenth century tavern owner had really begun to get the idea of how to run an agreeable hostellrie. Where, earlier, a big house would often be turned into an eatery in its owners' absence, the inn was now a proper, functioning entity in its own right. Smoking rooms, coffee rooms, dining rooms all had their place. Good plain cooking – cold meats, game pies, cheeses and pastries – were all on offer at a moment's notice and the tables were now laid properly with linen and china, rather than wood and pewter. A lady need not be ashamed to be seen eating at an inn on her journey.

England began to import French chefs, and grand ladies would compete over their pastry cooks and sauce chefs. After the French revolution English society lost many of its chefs, when they returned to France to open what we were to know as restaurants.

By the Edwardian era it began to be positively smart to dine out, and the amount one spent began to be an index of one's social status. This has not changed in the last seventy years: contemporary yuppies go to certain restaurants to prove how well they are doing, not how much they like good food.

As the restaurant began to figure more prominently in social life, so the restaurateur began to take on a new importance, a positive power in the hierarchy. The restaurant should be a place where food is cooked, served and cleared. It should not be a place of struggle and warfare.

In the best of all worlds, the waiter waits, the cook cooks, temperaments should not be allowed through the door. But the overbearing waiter plays a larger part than he should: while the cook's ego threatens to swallow up the customer's tentative preferences.

There are cooks who take their responsibilities too seriously. The great seventeenth-century chef Vatel killed himself with his kitchen knife because the sole did not arrive in time for a dinner given by Louis XIV, and in Wandsworth there is an angry young thug who decides that it is he, not the man who pays for his luxury, who knows what his customers really want.

History is replete with tales of eccentric gastro-entertainment. An American called C.G.K. Billings gave a 'horseback dinner' to thirty-six horsey friends to celebrate the opening of his $200,000 stable for thoroughbreds. He hired Sherry's ballroom and ruralised it with a background of rustic scenery, scattered with potted plants. The dance floor was covered with real sod

and the guests, dressed in white tie, ate from the backs of hacks hired from a livery stable. Trays were precariously attached to the pommels of the saddles, while the horses ate more comfortably from troughs filled with oats. The waiters, dressed in riding boots and hunting pink, had to sweep up the horses' droppings in between popping champagne corks.

Arnold Bennett, best known for his novels about the Potteries, wrote *The Grand Babylon Hotel* about the Savoy. First of all the reader is introduced to the real powers behind the Hotel: 'Next to the proprietor there were three gods at the hotel – Jules, the head waiter, Miss Spencer [in charge of the Bureau] and, most powerful of all, Rocco, the renowned chef, who earned two thousand a year and had a chalet on the Lake of Lucerne.' Theodore Racksole, the American millionaire, is brave enough to defy Jules himself. His first effrontery comes with his drink order:

> 'Bring me an Angel Kiss.'
> 'Pardon, sir?'
> 'Bring me an Angel Kiss, and be good enough to lose no time.'
> 'If it's an American drink, I fear we don't keep it, sir.' The voice of Jules fell icily distinct, and several men glanced around uneasily ...
> 'I didn't suppose you did keep it, but you can mix it, I guess, even in this hotel.'
> 'This isn't an American hotel, sir.' The calculated insolence of the words was cleverly masked beneath an accent of humble submission.

Racksole quietly goes off and buys the hotel before returning to the table and repeating his order.

Ludwig Bemelmanns describes the power of the *maître d'* in his book *Hotel Splendide*:

> Our tables – Nos. 81, 82 and 86 – were in a noisy, drafty corner of the balcony. They stood facing the stairs from the dining room and were between two doors. One door led to the pantry and was hung on whining hinges. On wet days it sounded like an angry cat and it was continually kicked by the boots of waiters rushing in and out with trays in their hands. The other door led to a linen closet

... Monsieur Victor used our tables as a kind of penal colony to which he sent guests who were notorious cranks, people who had forgotten to tip him over a long period of time and needed a reminder, undesirables who looked out of place in better sections of the dining room, and guests who were known to linger for hours over an order of *hors d'oeuvres* and a glass of milk while well-paying guests had to stand at the door waiting for a table.

Eating Out at Home and Abroad

It was recently mentioned in a book about the elusive Lord Lucan that every day for eighteen years he lunched on grilled lamb cutlets. The mind boggles. Of course I accept that there are nations which eat nothing other than rice, that whole tribes are reared on fufu or polenta, that every last inhabitant of some tropical island has yam (or is it breadfruit?) for breakfast, dinner, lunch and tea.

The difference between them and Lord Lucan is that he did it from choice. Each day he would go to the Clermont Club, wave aside the menu and say, 'I'll have the usual.' Oyster and prawns, lobster and crab, salmon smoked or fresh were all on offer. There was chicken and duck and game in season, pork and veal and beef and venison and, for people really hung up on sheep-meat, there was stewed lamb and reform cutlets and mixed grill (which included a lamb chop) and boiled mutton with caper sauce. But Lucan would have none of it.

There is something supremely British about 'having the usual'. It gives you a niche and, if overheard (and there really can be no point to asking for the usual unless you are overheard), it bestows upon you a certain authority, the air of being a man 'in the know'.

In the catering trade we have found that people are keener to let others know of their regular habits than they themselves are to perpetuate them. So when a client asks for 'the usual' and we forget what they had last time, anything is better than asking for particulars, no matter how much you apologise for your poor memory. Over the years I have rid myself of some very dubious liquor – like Van der Hum and Cordial Medoc – to people whom to the best of my knowledge I had never seen before, but who walked confidently up to the bar saying, 'Hello, Squire, I'll have the usual.'

On the whole the Englishman needs to gear himself up for a meal 'out'. He is going to ask a girl to marry him, or tell her to leave him. He is going to meet his brother or his daughter's fiancé. He needs something about which to talk to his business colleague apart from the fall of the dollar, and a menu will do as well as anything. He may need to impress a foreign visitor and an outing to a grand restaurant will, in his eyes, do that more than anything else. It is reasons of this kind which tempt an Englishman from his castle to face the inevitable dangers of foreign food.

Just about everyone is more open and relaxed in their attitude to restaurants and eating out than the English. To nearly every other culture it is a way of life, rather than a twice a year treat, which, statistically, is as often as the average Englishman eats out.

Of course it depends on where you live. Londoners have the world at their feet, but if you live in Durham there are precious few opportunities for fun food and on the whole the Englishman likes to play safe. He knows his local curry house, to which he will go after a drink or two, and he knows exactly which curry he can eat. Once he has discovered that chicken tikka massala is tasty and not too hot, that is what he will eat every time he crosses the threshold of the Royal Tandoori. Very occasionally he will splash out and have something else because it is cheaper and he is feeling poor – or possibly because it is more expensive and his ship has come in. Another place for bachelors is the local Chinese, but more often than not this involves a take-away rather than sitting down and eating. Truly good Chinese restaurants are not found outside major cities – London, of course, and Manchester, which has one of the best in England.

Englishmen tend not to take a girl to a curry house, unless the relationship is a long-established one, or the girl is about to be eased out of his life: what is called a Vindaloo farewell. The local wine bar is the place for women in good standing, where the quiches are soggy and the steak well-cooked. If there is no wine bar, there is bound to be an Italian restaurant within striking distance. Veal in white sauce with the odd mushroom in attendance or chicken cordon bleu, followed by the almost obligatory zabaglione. Small town French restaurants are often better, though usually more expensive than their Italian counterparts in which pasta and wine are filling, satisfactory *and* economical; older couples grow out of Italian and go back to French.

Restaurants in England have their biggest influx at Christmas. Late every afternoon streams of office workers in dishevelled suits conga back to the office wearing party hats and foolish smiles. Again, it is the Italian restaurants that reap most benefit from this annual lunacy. The office makes a deal with the restaurant – so many pounds a head, no more, liqueurs extra – and everyone relaxes. Many people never see the inside of a restaurant except in December.

When it comes to eating out Australians were even more backward than the English; for a long time they thought of food primarily as fuel rather than fun. An Aussie would never dream of looking at a restaurant for relaxation – only 'poofs' do that, they thought. So let's split a tube and get drunk. Maybe later we can drop in at Sheila's barbie.

Chinese cooking was the first to alert Australians to the idea of eating well and for pleasure, and from the mid-nineteenth century

on, stir-fried pork became an acceptable alternative to slabs of meat. Other ethnic food did not find a niche until almost a century later. Spaghetti and veal became smart in the sixties, *nouvelle cuisine* in the early and Vietnamese in the late seventies. In the eighties Aboriginal cooking is being given a turn, but this does not cheer up the Aborigines a lot. The Australians have also become aware that wine, which their vintners make ever more skilfully, is a good drink — and have put the can aside in favour of the bottle. All in all Australians are now happy to eat out for pleasure, and Sydney has among the best restaurants in the world.

The Japanese take almost everything seriously including restaurant life. They can spend as much on one meal as your showing-off yuppie might in a week — in the smartest 'Ryotei' between three and four hundred pounds a head is not all that unusual and they drink fine wine because it befits their station in life. In Japan high prices do not necessarily promise good food — just high status. Some of the cheaper restaurants are every bit as good and very much more fun.

In Hong Kong, too, good food is offered to friends or colleagues as a sign of respect. Competition between rival restaurants is fierce — and the punters participate in the atmosphere of feverish, if restrained, greed. Exotic fish and shellfish are kept in tanks by the restaurant door to tempt passers-by in, and it has been known for clients to gazump each other for the joy of eating a particularly juicy-looking sea-bass.

Italian food is possibly the most abused in England. With third-rate Italian restaurants in almost every market town, primarily because the food cost is low, the English country mouse could easily be forgiven for thinking Italian food is messy and uninteresting. Few Italians would put up with the standard they export. In Italy eating out is very much part of normal life, no matter what your age or income. Restaurant life is real life — you go out for something to eat, not to be seen. The Italians expect, and very often obtain, a high standard of cooking when they leave their homes for food.

The French probably go out less than the Italians, but they too expect and get good food, if it is only a steak-frites. They go to restaurants for business or significant family celebrations, but are much more relaxed about restaurant life than the English – because they understand food and wine; the menu is in their own language; no-one is trying to prove anything or hassle anyone – also service is included in the bill.

The Portuguese are also fairly relaxed – the waiters as much as the clients. Waiters in Portugal seem to enjoy their job more than anywhere else and will do most things for the client, from peeling an orange or propositioning your fiancée to taking the fish off the bone: this is helpful, for fish is an important element of the Portuguese diet.

You may think that America is not the place to go for a gastronomic holiday. You should think again. New Yorkers, who have always been secure in the knowledge that their city is the Mecca of good eating in the US, are having to work hard to outperform Los Angeles. The atmospheres in the two cities are still very different, though. New York is a walking city; LA is not. In New York, the restaurants are big, noisy and brightly lit, with display kitchens contributing to the theatricality of a night on the town. In Los Angeles, where the punters are more image-conscious, traditional French cooking has been hit by health freaks. Scandal, politics and films are joined by new restaurants as the most with-it subjects of conversation. One Los Angeles restaurant has installed closed-circuit television so that clients can see how their meal is progressing through the kitchen. Anything to keep the punters amused.

Ethnic Eating

My father was a great gourmand and suffered grievously from the results of rationing during the last world war. As hostilities ended, he hung a map of Europe on his study wall and kept a restaurant guide close at hand. Each time a country capitulated, or was liberated, he would look up establishments of that nationality, book a table and join the celebrations.

In the ensuing chapter I have tried to give a rough, simple-man's guide to the cuisines of the countries whose cooking you may find in Britain ... and tell you what are the specialities, when is the best time to go, what to look out for and also what to avoid.

There are many down market ethnic restaurants in Britain that serve English food; if you want to order eggs, chips and beans in a Chinese restaurant, so be it ... but the reason why you will like them there is probably that they run a decent establishment and you would enjoy their Wun Tun soup or chicken chow mein rather more. (What is certain is that if one of you wants ethnic, the other British, *they* cook our way with more grace and more skill than *we* do it theirs.)

Many people believe that if you go to, say, a Korean restaurant and see it full of Koreans it must be authentic and of high quality. Not true ... any more than if you go to an English restaurant and find it full of Englishmen it is necessarily good. What is true is that people in foreign lands, bewildered by strange customs and incomprehensible language, like to relax with people of their own culture ... hence Poles in Polish tea-rooms, Americans in MacDonalds.

Let me remind the reader who is considering visiting an ethnic restaurant in Britain that it is *they* who have come to *us*; it is therefore less than essential to do heavy homework into the gastro-culture of the country whose fare you are to sample. I consider it the height of discourtesy to have menus printed in a language not spoken by the indigenous clientèle unless dishes are clearly translated.

There are many Britons who feel that if they speak loudly enough, foreigners will understand and they have used this system around the world; it has, on the whole, given us a bad name, but what is certain is that if you take a little trouble to find out about the national traditions of the ethnic restaurant you intend to visit, you will do better than the average schmuck who goes in with a feeling of distrust and deep suspicion.

The odd phrase in a foreign language, such as is provided in the ensuing chapter, is *not* so that they will understand that you want the bill, the loo, to say hello or goodbye (those are actually the first words of English they are taught). It is to show that you have worked a bit on being a good ethnic customer — implying the desire that they will take pains to ensure that your studies have been worthwhile. Speaking the odd word of a foreign language is a signal of good will — no more. In practice, you are likely to mispronounce the words, use the wrong form of address, mistake the tense, generally look an ass.

I had a friend who spent many years running Reuters in Peking. When he came back to London he took me to a Chinese restaurant and did a fluent three-minute monologue in Cantonese, saying words to the effect that I, his guest, was a famous gourmet, he the host a knowledgeable consumer of the provincial cuisines of the waiter's motherland. When he ended this speech, the waiter looked at him in puzzlement and said, 'You speakee Chinese.' It is like in America where, when you tell a joke without prefacing it with 'This is a joke', no one laughs.

You will find over the next pages much information, some of it unlikely to be very useful (like the Korean for 'That was disgusting'), but a few pertinent words in *their* language gives the diner the edge ... and giving diners the edge is exactly what this book is aiming to achieve.

Greeting: Bonjour at lunch time, *bonsoir* in the evening, followed by the gender of the person you are greeting. If in doubt, look into the middle distance and say, 'Monsieur/dame'.

Food Likely to be Served: Rich sauces, cream-influenced in the north and garlic-influenced in the south. Vegetables are served as a separate course, and cheese is served before pudding so that red wine can continue to be drunk. The French are less particular about the temperature of the food than the English.

Typical Dishes to Confound Visitors: Snails in garlic butter, served in their shells (*escargots*), frogs' legs (*cuisses de grenouilles*), forked like little ballerinas and tasting vaguely chickeny. *Tête de veau* is literally a calf's head and *boudin* is black pudding, often served with fried apples and boiled potatoes.

National Traits: The French are very serious (*très sérieux*) about their food.

Good Dishes for the Unadventurous: Poulet de Bresse Rôti is corn-fed roast chicken. *Filet de sole bonne femme* is Dover sole in a white wine and mushroom sauce.

Asking for the Bill: Call the waiter '*Monsieur*' or '*garçon*'. Ask for *la compte, l'addition* or *la note*. Scribbling gestures in the air also work.

That was Excellent: C'était vraiment excellent.

That was Disgusting: C'était dégoûtant or *immangeable.*

Good Days to Go: July 14th – the storming of the Bastille, when they did away with their monarchy so that they now make do with denigrating ours. October 26th – Mitterand's birthday. They probably won't know that in the restaurant, but may offer you a brandy (*une fine*) if you tell them.

Trendy Drinks: Pernod before the meal, *marc de Bourgogne* after it.

Goodbye: Au revoir if you mean to return, *adieu* if not.

Greeting: Buon giorno at lunch, *buona sera* in the evening.

Food Likely to be Served: Veal and liver (both cut into strips unless you specifically ask for it otherwise). *Bollito misto* – literally 'mixed boiled' – is boiled chicken, beef, garlic sausage and veal served in a soup plate with the broth. At its best it has two sensational sauces – one tomato, anchovy, garlic and oil, the other mixed herbs, chopped onion and oil. Pasta comes with as many different shapes and sauces as there are Italian towns and is often served as a first course. So is risotto. Italian risotto rice is closer to our pudding rice than long grain. Risottos vary almost as much as pasta: one covered with grated white truffle is out of this world (also ruinously expensive). The best Italian cheeses are Parmesan (avoid the sawdust in cardboard containers which goes under that name) and gorgonzola (a blue cheese). Italian puddings are sweet dry cakes or ice-creams, which are the best in the world.

Typical Dishes to Confound Visitors: Osso bucco. The marrow bones are stewed and you eat the marrow as well as the bone's residual flesh. *Fritto misto* is no fun if you cannot (or think you cannot) eat brains. Brains, cauliflower, liver and onion are dipped in batter and fried to a golden crispness.

National Traits: Relaxed and good-humoured. The Italians have less pomposity about their food than the French, and are very, very keen on children.

Good Dishes for the Unadventurous: Veal *milanese*, an escalope of veal coated in breadcrumbs and fried, served with a wedge of lemon. Lasagne is much more delicious in Italy than in most English places, although the idea is the same – layers of flat pasta with white sauce and meat sauce between each layer. Spaghetti is also better in the country of its creation – *napoletana* is with tomato sauce and *bolognese* is with meat sauce. Very few people know that spaghetti are the insides of macaroni so there has to be a relationship in the sales of these two pastas.

Asking for the Bill: Il conto per favore.

That was Excellent: Era delizioso or just *ottimo*.
That was Disgusting: Era schifoso (skeefoso).

Good Days to Go: Almost any saint's day. Tell the owner that you have the same name as the saint in question and he will help you celebrate. 25th April is Liberation Day, 15th August the Day of the Assumption, 1st November All Saints' Day, 8th December Immaculate Conception.

What to Drink: Chianti is making a comeback, though no longer in a wicker-covered bottle. *Valpolicella* is pleasant and light, sometimes *pétillant* (with a hint of a fizz). A sub-culture called *Amarone* is wondrously alcoholic and smooth with it. Italian liqueurs are of doubtful virtue, although old timers still drink *strega*, a yellow aniseed-based drink that gives lasting hangovers. *Grappa* is the Italian equivalent of *marc* – a spirit made of the must (pips and skins of grapes). It is alcoholic and trendy.

Goodbye: Arrivaderla if you are formal, *arrivaderci* if less so, and *ciao* (chow) if you know the people well or all their shirt buttons are undone.

Service is usually included in the bill, but you will want to add extra because the people are so nice. If you want to insult an Italian waiter by insinuating he is a homosexual, pull your earlobe as you look at him. This is to be used only in cases of extreme provocation and if you are bigger than he is – Italians don't mind being blamed for being poor soldiers, but become furious at accusations that they are anything but brilliant heterosexual lovers.

Greeting: Yiasou.

Food Likely to be Served: Chicken, fish and lamb dishes. Often-seen vegetables are aubergines, onions and tomatoes. Tarama-solata is a popular starter – smoked cod's roe beaten with olive oil and often cream or yoghurt. Rice wrapped in vine leaves and fish salads are other good starters. It is often a sound idea to eat a meal made up of many first courses rather than moving on to a main course. Fish dishes are common, usually with inter-esting garlicked sauces. Lamb with lemon and spinach is many people's favourite, and *avgalemono* – a chicken and lemon soup – is, at its best, sensational. Puddings tend to be very sweet honey and almond pastry cakes. Cheeses, notably feta, are sharp and unsubtle.

Typical Dishes to Confound Visitors: Octopi cooked in their ink, which are delicious, but strong-tasting and bitter.

National Traits: The Greeks are very ebullient and hospitable, although they no longer encourage you to break plates.

Good Dishes for the Unadventurous: Moussaka – everything a cottage pie should be and could be if we marinated the meat and added herbs before mincing it. Layers of minced lamb and aubergine and onion and tomatoes are topped with a thick panada which browns while sealing the flavours underneath. If that is too foreign, there will be plenty of charcoal cooked chicken or kebabs – skewered meat and peppers – on the menu.

Asking for the Bill: Logariasmo.

That was Excellent: Oreo.

That was Disgusting: Abesion.

Good Days to Go: 25th March – Annunciation, 6th August – Saviour's Day, 15th August – Assumption, and at New Year.

What to Drink: Retsina, a strong tasting wine flavoured in resinous barrels. Greek house wines will be fine, and should be cheap. It is always better to drink cheap red than cheap white.

Goodbye: Yiasou.

Greek cooking can be greasy, over-lemoned or over-garlicked and indigestible. It can also be excellent if the ingredients are fresh and the cooking light-handed.

TURKISH

Greeting: Merhaba.

Food Likely to be Served: Turkish and Greek cuisine are so closely related that even the Turks have difficulty in defining the differences. Herbs and spices are used, but the main flavours will be garlic and olive oil, with a fair amount of yoghurt thrown in for luck. Courgettes, aubergines and pimentos all feature, while the main meat used is lamb – minced, chopped, grilled or stewed. Fish is eaten a great deal in Turkey itself, but is not seen so often in Turkish restaurants in London – the Turks find it too hard to acquire enough fresh Mediterranean fish. Grilled red mullet is popular and delicious as well as pretty. Puddings are sticky and sweet – *paklava* is a crispy pastry stuffed with nuts and honey, *kadief* are like shredded wheat, also with nuts and honey.

Typical Dishes to Confound the Visitor: You have to be very suspicious of foreign food to worry in a Turkish restaurant, but those who think yoghurt ought only to be eaten at breakfast may be distressed by *yourgutlu kebab* – minced lamb chopped on pitta bread with a tomato and garlic sauce and smothered in yoghurt.

National Traits: The waiters are often disagreeably flirtatious.

Good Dishes for the Unadventurous: Kebabs. *Adala kebab* is marinated lamb grilled over charcoal. The Turkish moussaka has a more winy bechamel than the Greek variety. And of course the sish kebab (skewered lamb) is an old favourite.

Asking for the Bill: Hesaplutsen.

That was Excellent: Mukennel.

That was Disgusting: Pek iyi degil.

Good Days to Go: Bayram – two days in August (movable feast). A religious festival celebrated by drinking as much as possible.

What to Drink: Almost anything but Turkish wines. Again, cheap whites are even nastier than cheap reds. Turkish cherry juice is popular and excellent.

Goodbye: Allahaismarladik.

LEBANESE

Greeting: Mahaba.

Food Likely to be Served: Lots of appetisers, known as *meze*. You should find radishes, cucumber and chilli waiting on your table for you to pick at as you decide upon your order. *Humous* (sieved chickpeas) and mashed aubergine and *falafel* (which is a sort of bean-burger) are commonly found on Lebanese menus, as are stuffed vine leaves. Soups have a low profile and are made of pulses – lentil is good. The dressing for vegetables and salads and pickles is either thickened yoghurt called *labne* or olive oil and lemon juice and garlic. Puddings are syrupy and laced with nuts and honey.

Typical Dishes to Confound Visitors: A great deal of offal appears on a Lebanese menu – brain, tongue, liver and spleen – which is confined to haggis in countries in which it is not processed into moist pet-food.

National Traits: Lebanese waiters often behave as though their duties do not, and should not, extend to civility simply because someone is a customer. You do tend to get the service you deserve.

Good Dishes for the Unadventurous: The meat dishes are all fairly unadventurous: lamb, chicken and fish grilled over charcoal or stuffed with rice.

Asking for the Bill: Laheb or *fatura.*

That was Excellent: Tir payeb.

That was Disgusting: Mish mnegh with the last sound hissed.

Good Days to Go: 15th August – the Feast of St Mary.

What to Drink: Arak, which is an aniseed-flavoured spirit. Turkish coffee, drunk after the meal, is very thick and strong. If you don't like sugar, tell the waiter, as the coffee must be sweetened as it is made . . . and is very sweet unless you explain.

Goodbye: Masselemeh.

JEWISH

Greeting: Shalom.

Food Likely to be Served: Chopped chicken liver, with onion and chicken fat and chopped hard-boiled egg is a very Jewish dish, as is salt beef, served with rye bread and no butter. (Do not expect butter or creamy sauces: religious dietary laws forbid the consumption of meat and dairy products at the same meal.) Tongue is popular, as is *borscht* (beetroot soup) and barley soup. *Lockshen* pudding, which is like rice pudding made of noodles, and *apfel strudel* are also part of Jewish cuisine. Pickled cucumbers, *heimische* (with garlic), rye bread and a relish of beetroot and horseradish is excellent. Their frankfurters – made from beef – do miss the smack you get from a pork sausage.

Typical Dishes to Confound Visitors: Stuffed neck, which is much tastier than it sounds.

National Traits: The waiters are larger than life, prone to telling you what *not* to eat. They consider that it is their job to cheer you up and make you feel cared for.

Good Dishes for the Unadventurous: Latkes, which are potato cakes, and *kreplach*, which are dumplings.

Asking for the Bill: Heshbon or *cabala* (asking for a receipt).

That was Excellent: Hayah metzuyan.

That was Disgusting: 'Things haven't changed, then.'

Good Days to Go: Passover. Or any Saturday evening when the Sabbath is over (after dark). Don't go on Yom Kippur, the Day of Atonement.

What to Drink: There is not a lot of alcohol, which keeps down the overall price of the meal but makes food expensive. Russian tea, apple juice or cold beetroot juice are the main drinks. Wine is allowed, Israeli wine being sweet and of no great quality.

Goodbye: Shalom.

Thank You: Todar aba.

INDIAN

Greeting: Ohe or *ashung* (although thanks to the Raj 'Good evening' will do).

Food Likely to be Served: Curries. Which have come on a long way since the days when a piece of meat was rolled in curry powder and cooked. There is a great deal of vegetarian cooking now: vegetarian thali – a whole dish of lentil, bean, occra, potato and pea curries – is delicious. Meat thalis – dishes of meat curries, kebabs and tandooris – are also becoming popular. Side dishes are very important in Indian cookery: *nan* or *naan* — leavened bread baked in a tandoori oven, oval and sometimes sprinkled with sesame seed. *Chapati* — round, unleavened bread cooked in a grill. *Popadom* (spiced or plain) are made of lentil flour and deep fried in very hot fat, which makes them puff up a bit. *Samosas* (also eaten as a starter with a minty sauce) are triangles of batter-dough filled with meat or vegetables and deep fried. *Dhals* are stewed pulses — usually lentils. Mango chutney no longer only comes from Sharwoods, and is often made in the restaurant. Unripe mangoes are cut into fine strips and marinated with lime and tamarind — crunchy and excellent. The curries themselves vary a great deal according to which part of India they come from. *Kormas* are mild and creamy, with fruit and nuts. *Moghlai* are also mild curries involving many spices, yoghurts, creams and heavily reduced milk. *Birianis* are mild curries which come ready dressed with rice. Parsee cooking involves flavours like coriander and ginger and can be interesting and good.

Typical Dishes to Confound Visitors: Anything calling itself a *Phaal* is a very hot curry indeed. *Vindaloo* is only for the strong palated, and *Madras* curries are probably the spiciest most Englishmen can take.

National Traits: Indian waiters are usually very gentle and civilised, often over-qualified for the job they do. Almost unfailingly courteous.

Good Dishes for the Unadventurous: Tandoori chicken — mildly spiced and baked in a special tandoori oven — with a vegetable side dish (*sag* is spinach). King prawns lightly fried in batter are an easy way to start the meal.

Asking for the Bill: Bill or *bill den.*

That was Excellent: Khub valo.

That was Disgusting: Valo na.

Good Days to Go: Eid – celebrating the end of Ramadan, a big day in the Muslim calendar. If your restaurant is Hindu, try *Puja* – the goddess's festival, a movable feast.

What to Drink: Lager is the best idea. Most curries would overwhelm most wines.

Goodbye: Dekahabe.

Thank You: Dahnabad.

THAI

Greeting: Sawa dee ka.

Food Likely to be Served: Thai food resembles a spicy Chinese cuisine – closest to Szechuan cooking. Thai soups are thickened with coconut cream and are redolent of lemon grass, garlic and spices. Coriander is a spice often used in the Thai kitchen. Food is cooked in a wok – fish often overcooked. Thai cooking makes more of the sauce than of the ingredient it is to accompany.

Typical Dishes to Confound Visitors: Anything which says 'Prik' will include chilli and be very hot. Whole cloves of garlic often appear in your mouth. *Nam-prik* is a sauce made of fish sauce (the Thai equivalent to soy), dried shrimps, chilli, garlic, lime juice and tamarind. It is served with all the titbits which accompany a Thai meal.

National Traits: Thai restaurant staff are very pleasant though less technical (more forgetful) than the Japanese.

Good Dishes for the Unadventurous: Satay – chicken or beef spiced, skewered and grilled and served with a crushed peanut sauce. Almost a nursery taste.

Asking for the Bill: Get wen dweka.

That was Excellent: Aloi maaka.

That was Disgusting: Mai aloika.

Good Days to Go: 12th August – Queen's birthday.

What to Drink: Cold Thai beer (*Singha*), iced tea or white wine.

Goodbye. Baigonaka.

INDONESIAN

Greeting: Selamat fiang for early evening; *selamat malam* at night. They may reply *selamat makam*, which means 'enjoy your food'.

Food Likely to be Served: A mixture of the Chinese and Indian approaches to food. *Rijsttafel* is the Dutch East Indies' feast with a mountain of coloured rice surrounded by side dishes – spiced meat and fish and vegetables, locally about as popular as memories of Dutch colonial rule. *Satay* is also found – skewered meat served with peanut sauce. *Laksa* is a coconut based soup, with so many things floating around in it it is as complete a meal as an Irish stew. *Kare kambing* is an acceptable lamb curry. Banana fritters make a good pudding and are called *pisang goreng. Opor ayam* is chicken cooked in coconut milk.

Typical Dishes to Confound Visitors: Gado gado, which sounds delicious but is a vegetable salad. Beef rendang is extremely hot.

National Traits: The staff will come in all shades from kindness to truculence.

Good Dishes for the Unadventurous: Nasi goreng – fried rice with bits in it.

That was Excellent: Baik baik sekali.

That was Disgusting: Tidak bagus.

Good Days to Go: Lebaran or *Hriraya* – movable feasts in May, after Ramadan.

What to drink: Cold beer – *bintang*. Or tea. Or sweetened water – *air*. Unsweetened water is *air puti*.

Goodbye: Selamat malam.

CHINESE

Greeting: Ni hao.

Food Likely to be Served: Cantonese cookery is the most common in England; Szechuan/Peking the most flavoursome. Soups are usually clear and can taste of anything from washing up water to rich consommé. Hot and sour soup is just that. *Wun tun* are like ravioli, filled with forcemeat. In Cantonese restaurants look for black bean sauce which is highly flavoured and served with beef. Beef with oyster sauce is another popular dish. Crispy-skinned Peking duck, served with pancakes, thinly sliced cucumber and spring onions and *hoysin* (spiced plum) sauce is a great delicacy. (Everything is wrapped in the pancake and eaten like a spring roll.) *Dim-sum* (Chinese dumplings) are flavoured with almost anything from crab to oysters and most other fish; with pork, vegetables or green ginger. Bean curd is Cantonese and eaten fried or steamed and served with prawns or scallops. Steamed scallops with ginger are delicious. Tea leaf and camphor-wood smoked duck is excellent. You will find puddings in Szechuan restaurants, not Cantonese. Banana and apple fritters are best.

Typical Dishes to Confound Visitors: Shark's fin soup is gelatinous, horribly expensive, and more of a ritual than a good dish. Bang bang chicken is hot, peppery and served cold. Deep fried seaweed is not seaweed, so there is no point in trying to cook your own from the shore. It is kale or spring greens, finely shredded and fried. (Seaweed subjected to deep fat turns into blobs of goo.)

National Traits: Inscrutability and subservience that comes across as downright rudeness. As most Chinese restaurant staff put all the money they have on horses and greyhounds, an acceptable tip is Trap 5 in the fourth race at Hackney rather than 10%.

Good Dishes for the Unadventurous: Chicken and sweetcorn soup, followed by sweet and sour pork with boiled rice.

Asking for the Bill: Gei quianba.

That was Excellent: Haojile.

That was Disgusting: Bu hao chi.

Good Days to Go: Chinese New Year, which moves each year within January and February. Most Chinese restaurants hold special feasts on that day and include visitors in their celebration. October 1st – National Day, used as an excuse to have fun.

What to Drink: There are many different kinds of delicious Chinese tea: lychee tea is brilliant, mango tea exciting but green tea the most refreshing. If you want to drink alcohol, try *Sake* – rice wine which is served hot – or stick to dry house white or lager, followed by a highly alcoholic 'schnapps' called *Mao Tai.*

Goodbye: Zaijian.

KOREAN

Greeting: Annog hashnika.

Food Likely to be Served: Beef, fish and soyabean are the main components of Korean cooking, which is a very simple version of other oriental cooking. It is served less highly spiced in a restaurant than it would be in a Korean home, but some of the dishes are strong tasting. Noodles and rice and black beans also figure highly. The 'feasts' figuring on the menu are substantial and good value.

Typical Dishes to Confound Tourists: Kim-Chee is a fermented vegetable pickle which is strong on garlic and chilli. (Koreans used to eat it with silver chopsticks which became discoloured when the food was poisoned.)

National Traits: Korean waiters are warmer than the Japanese, nicer than the Chinese and are very happy to advise you when you order. They laugh a great deal in a friendly way.

Good Dishes for the Unadventurous: Bulogi, the national dish, is strips of marinated beef grilled – often at table by the waitress. Puddings are, as elsewhere in Eastern cooking, very sweet and sticky.

Asking for the Bill: Kirhan so.

That was Excellent: Mashi yfsneeda.

That was Disgusting: Mashi oxyneeda.

Good Days to Go: New Year's Day and Korean New Year's Day, a movable feast in February. August 15th – Independence Day.

What to Drink: Jung jung is the Korean version of rice wine. It is more aromatic than sake. Sadly there is no drink called Freud Freud and Adler Adler would only get you two typewriters. Ginseng, which supposedly does everything from cure warts to increase life expectancy and sexual potency is also popular. Barley tea is served the way we serve water but is not very good.

Goodbye: Amnong hee karseyoh.

JAPANESE

Greeting: Domo.

Food Likely to be Served: Sushi, thumb-shaped envelopes of vinegared glutinous short-grained rice with raw fish wrapped in nori seaweed. *Yakitori* is chunks of skewered chicken with a rich glazed sauce. *Shabu shabu* is a main dish, paper-thin slices of beef, vegetables and beancurd cooked in light stock. Drink the stock after you have eaten although you will have to ask to do so, else it will disappear with the waiter.

Typical Dishes to Confound Visitors: Sashimi: the famous raw fish dish, cut into beautiful patterns. The more intricate the pattern, the more highly your host respects you, but you have to be knowledgeable to recognise the degree of compliment intended.

National Traits: Only some Japanese drink in their country, but when they do — especially Black Label whisky — they get very drunk indeed. *Sake* and premium whiskies are their favourites — currently Chivas Regal is the 'in' Scotch. Even when drunk the Japanese are scrupulously polite.

Good Dishes for the Unadventurous: Tempura (a Portuguese import) — morsels of food (mussels, occra, oysters, prawns) cooked in batter and fried to golden deliciousness. Ask for a variety of vegetables lightly cooked in soy. If you don't want to try new things, try not to go to a Japanese restaurant.

Asking for the Bill: Okanjyo onegai shimasu.

That was Excellent: Oishikatta.

That was Disgusting: Mazukatta, but no Japanese would dream of saying anything so rude.

Good Days to Go: During Golden Week, in April/May. This is a feast revering ancestors and young people.

What to Drink: Sake — rice wine, drunk warm. Whisky — they have a Japanese *Suntory* which is not bad. Anything less alcoholic than these is a waste of good drinking time. Never fill your own wine-cup: others will keep it filled for you. Shout 'Campai' ('Dry your little wine-cup') as you drink. They have recently taken to Dry Beer which has high alcohol, low sugar and is a very voguey lager.

Goodbye: Sayonara.

Atmosphere

I often get asked whether food, drink, value for money or atmosphere is the most important factor of an enjoyable meal. It is my contention that you need all four.

A bad atmosphere will destroy a delicious meal; but it is possible to enjoy an indifferent meal if the atmosphere is good enough. For instance, at Langan's Brasserie in London there is a steady stream of well-known diners, amazingly confident waiters, attractive and efficient receptionists. When you are served a plate of run-of-the-mill smoked salmon, as we were the other day, you tend to say, 'What the hell, I'm having a good time.' But if the vibes are wrong – if the welcome is grudging, the waiter offensive, the atmosphere one of church-like whispering, the best food in the world will not cheer you up.

That archetypal complaint about a meal 'If the soup had been as hot as the champagne and the champagne as old as the chicken and the chicken as fat as the waiter it would have been all right' has stood the test of time for it embraces food, drink and service, the pillars of a good meal. The right atmosphere is brought about by a mixture of good decor, honest approach to the clientèle and, most important of all, a lack of cant: being at home with what you are selling. That means calling food by its actual name rather than some appellation culled from the *Repertoire de la Cuisine* which the customer can't understand and the chef cannot cook. It means food and drink are respected but *not* revered, for a restaurant is a place of enjoyment, not worship.

Cleanliness is good, overt hygiene gives the impression that they spend their time buying detergent and cleaning rather than marketing and cooking.

Background music – at the right level – is all right when the place is empty, but unnecessary when it is full, for the buzz of uninhibited conversation creates the best atmosphere and is the best music by which to enjoy a good meal.

Most important of all, the enjoyment of the customer must come before the seriousness of the catering operation. There must be a ratio between the quality of the food and the number of people who come along and ask you to comment on it; if a punter is eating heartily there is no need to ask him whether things are all right. If you are *not* eating, then you *should* be asked if anything is wrong. If no one approaches you, do not leave a tip.

Decor

The caterer has two quite separate headings for his expenditure: food and drink and cigars, which he buys – and sells at a profit; decor and software and furnishing of lavatories, which is an investment to bring in the clientèle who will spend money and make his fortune. A restaurateur, too mean to spend money on a well-equipped and good-looking loo, tends not – and does not deserve – to make a profit.

Restaurants like their customers to be comfortable enough to want to sit and eat, but not so comfortable that they don't move on once the productive part of the meal is over. Settling back and ordering vast quantities of food and wine is a Good Thing. Talking and smoking, which makes no money for the establishment, is a Bad Thing.

In places where the average 'spend' is over £25 a head, it is understood that the client will stay for up to three hours, so a table booked for 7.30 will be re-allocated for 10.30 although the customer will of course not be told. It is up to the restaurant to make him feel that it is time he left.

In cheaper restaurants, the owner will want the turnover to be a bit faster – hence the popularity of bent-wood chairs, bought not so that the punters will cry 'What pretty turn of the century furniture' but because it strains their arses to sit in them for any great length of time.

A restaurant will cram as many chairs and tables into a space as it can fit, and with which the kitchen can cope. A restaurant with a feeling of space about it is not designed that way to ensure the punters can have a private conversation without being overheard; it is like that either because they don't have a lot of trade (and it is better to have six full tables and a queue than fifteen half-empty tables) or because the kitchen cannot deal with a greater flow of clients than will fit around what is on offer in the way of seating.

Round tables are a luxury in that they take up more floor-space than square ones and cannot be pushed together to make room for large parties. The best restaurants have a mixture of both shapes, only stupid ones have round tables only.

If the table legs are uneven and the table rocks, don't think that the management is not aware of the fact and that the table hasn't been rocking for years. It is perfectly possible to buy gadgets to lengthen and stabilise table-legs and if they have not bought them, it must be for some good reason: tip accordingly. Use a knife under the shortest leg; it will not hurt the knife greatly, but usually brings the staff along with an alternative.

Napkins should bear some relation to the price of the meal: linen napkins are *de rigueur* if the cost is more than £25 a head, but if it is less than £10 a head, economies are acceptable; washing and ironing napkins is quite expensive.

Cutlery is more important to the enjoyment of a meal than some establishments seem to realise . . . many otherwise excellent restaurants have cheap cutlery, as they think the more expensive the knives and forks the more likely are they to be stolen by staff and customers (everyone knows and accepts that teaspoons are stolen).

Smart restaurants provide large glasses, which inhibits a party of six from ordering only one bottle of wine. Decent restaurants have glasses of different sizes and there is as little reason for not asking for a different sized glass as for a different sized bottle. Beware of tulip-shaped liqueur glasses which contain 50% of the drink in the last (top) centimetre of the glass. You can make some good money on bets with that piece of information. Ask someone to fill the glass half way. Pour that into a wine glass. Then you pour what you think is a half full glass – to about a half-centimetre from the brim – pour that into the wine glass and then ask people what they think will happen if you pour the contents of the wine glass into the tulip glass.

Lighting is important to both the customer and the waiter. The room should be dark enough to be discreet, light enough for a short-sighted person to read a menu. And not quite so light as to let people read the prices without looking most carefully. If punters are not comfortable with the lighting, they will not return.

The more notices in and around a restaurant, the less competent is its management. The name of the place outside should be enough for anyone to find it. Plastic waiters standing on the pavement with a pointing finger, lights that flash on and off, radio commercials (unless the restaurant is new), sandwich men, leafleteers – all these are signs of failure. A really successful restaurant does not even need to display its name over the door – Le Gavroche can now be found in the phone book but used to be ex-directory. Too much advertising means that customers have been once and are not coming back. 'No coach parties' does not mean a thing as the offending vehicle can be parked around the corner and decant its load into the restaurant in pairs. 'No van-dwellers', a notice written on the doors of many pubs in East Anglia, is illegal, but still appears.

A sensible restaurant will have a public telephone if only to

stop people from bringing mobile phones in with them. It is not everyone's idea of fun to dine with a telephone ringing at the next table.

More and more restaurants have 'No Smoking' zones. I wish they did not. Smoke is offensive to many people, especially when they are eating good food. There are also those who cannot manage without a cigarette, and they have just as much right to a happy life. *Why cannot there be specific smoking areas?* Then those who smoke would be identified as the kinks, rather than those of us who don't being made to feel like social lepers. Lavatory doors are marked LAVATORY; all other doors are not marked THIS IS NOT A LAVATORY.

Uniforms

When I worked at the Dorchester Hotel the single most magnificent thing about the place was the carriage attendant. He was tall and wore a grey and gold uniform with white gloves on his hands while upon his head was perched a top hat spangled with gold braid, matched by that which adorned the sides of his trousers. He had gold embroidered oak leaves on his shoulders and a medal gained in some long forgotten battle sparkled on his chest. His cousins opened car doors at all the great hotels in the metropolis and once I asked him why he and his fellow attendants were all so magnificently dressed. Surely, I ventured, it would be easier to open car doors in overalls and dark gloves. 'It's the tips, boy,' he said. 'Seeing all that gold makes them embarrassed to leave under a shilling.'

I doubt that there is any better reason for *any* of the clothes worn in the catering industry.

In the beginning, when it was a real case of 'them and us', waiters were of so low a class that they could not be depended upon to own clothes suitable for making contact with the great ... so they were issued with poor imitations of suits worn by their betters: dinner jackets with white ties; tail suits with black ties; monkey jackets; plastic dickies; celluloid collars; made up bow ties and, for the lowly commis, huge white aprons over dark trousers – about the most unsuitable uniform imaginable for racing down stairs and panting back up loaded with silver trays and dishes. After the 1940s, partly because of clothes rationing and partly because of the beginning of the collapse of the social divide, waiters began to wear clothes slightly more suited to their actual job ... soft collars and maroon jackets with gold buttons over dress shirts and bow ties. But whatever they wore one of the reasons was to intimidate.

Chefs wear white ... *the* most unsuitable colour for a kitchen that deals in green herbs, brown sauces, tomato coulis and fat that might be invisible if splashed over garments of other colours. They wear hats – originally so that hair did not fall into the food – for the heat and humidity of kitchens is conducive to falling hair; white hats are now worn to denote rank – taller the hat, bigger the job – and it is *very helpful* to know that a man dressed like that is the chef, so that you can speak to him and treat him as such. Men in morning coats, tail suits and dinner jackets are not necessarily restaurant staff. (I once tipped the Earl of Mountbatten two shillings, mistaking him for the *maître d'* in a dimly lit night club.)

Dress

When you go out to a restaurant dress in whatever makes you feel comfortable. If the restaurant won't accept you, it is unlikely you would have been comfortable there. It is different if you are a guest; people who invite others to expensive restaurants are rare enough and it would be dumb to embarrass them.

Restaurants like their customers to dress well, because they have this mistaken idea that well dressed people don't make scenes — and more than anything else restaurateurs hate scenes; they are bad for business. People dressed for Royal Ascot don't make scenes. It is rare for folk in dinner jackets to cause bovver, but punters in designer jeans and open necked shirts make them apprehensive; at the same time they quite like badly dressed customers as they make the waiter's clothes look that much less tacky.

Sometimes the restaurant will try to lend you a tie or jacket so that you are in their debt. Do not accept their clothes. In the long run most restaurants will let in anyone provided they pay . . . although they might put you into an obscure corner.

The safest thing to do — if you like casual clothes and are not quite sure whether they have sartorial house rules — is to keep a jacket and tie in your car and put them on if the waiters are stroppy, and you decide nevertheless that you want to eat there.

The Menu

In my opinion the very best sort of menu gives you choices in each section – starter, main dish, sweet/savoury at a price set against the main dish. It should also tell you how much a selection will cost – with one price for two courses, another for three and another for four. *What I hate* is when this nearly happens – only lots of items are marked £2 extra: there is nothing more inhibiting for guests than to have to subject their hosts to '£2 extra' orders, nothing more irritating for the host either. A restaurant does not have to charge more for smoked salmon than for smoked mackerel – it can just give a smaller serving of the more expensive dish. There was a time when we restaurateurs thought it smart to give only the host the menu with prices. This meant a guest would say, 'May I have a veal escalope' and the host (the only one to know that veal escalope cost £12.50) could say, 'I don't really recommend it, try the lamb cutlets.' The Connaught Hotel in London now has the best menu pricing system. The price of the main dish – £32.50 for roasted wild duck – includes any first course and any cheese or pudding. And at the bottom of the menu is a list of 'extras' like foie gras and oysters and parma ham – so if you want an extra, you have an extra course and pay the asking price.

Table d'hôte means a pre-described set meal, at a set price, usually with one or two choices in each course. Soup or fruit cocktail. Lamb, skate or omelette. Sweet or cheese.

A la carte means that you order what you want from anywhere you like on the menu. There is usually (and should be) a note about the minimum charge, otherwise people could order a soup and roll and butter and cheese and make the restaurant the net losers (which is not the point of the exercise) on the outing. *But* provided what you order comes up to the minimum charge, there is no reason on earth why you should not ask for three starters, or a main dish and four puddings if that is what you fancy.

Two good reasons for menus are: to make the proprietor feel prouder about the food on offer — *salmis de pintade provençale* sounds classier than stewed Guinea fowl with garlic — and to tell the customer lies about what he is going to eat by making ordinary food sound special. You can also score via inverted snobbery, like in Dartmouth where there is a splendid restaurant called the Carved Angel, and 'Offal' features on the menu. Because it is a famous eatery with stars and gongs and chefs' cloches and suchlike, you order the offal and get all the best of what the Americans call 'variety meats', like calves' liver, lambs' kidney and sheep's brains. Elsewhere you would ask, 'What offal?' lest they present you with a plate of ox hearts and beef kidney.

Of secondary importance to the reasons for having a menu, is to tell the customer what there is to eat and how much it will cost. There are non-words on menus — delicious, succulent. In fact any qualitative assessment is dishonest for it is the consumer, not the supplier, whose judgement of food is material.

Menus are not cookbooks. They are there to describe the end product, not teach you how to make it: raw monkfish passed through a hair-sieve by a lady of easy virtue, blended with raw egg white into which Jersey cream is folded prior to simmering in a *court bouillon* may be true, but it is too much if you are going to eat the dish and not enough if you want to go home and cook it. It is a very understandable thing for a caterer to want to confuse the customer and make him think that it is astonishingly complicated to produce what he has on offer (it usually is not). At the same time it is absolutely right for customers to go to restaurants and eat something which is tricky to make at home — like deep fried camembert which often leaks into the deep fat so that you have to sieve the fat pan and start from scratch. What is nutty is for people to go to restaurants and order what they can do better at home — like joints of meat.

There should be a brief description of the dishes on offer, with especial mention of when garlic, curry powder, chilli, coriander or items to which some people take violent exception are used in cooking.

When we had the *ancienne cuisine*, the chefs were taught by The Book, and The Book was *Le Repertoire de la Cuisine*. It contained every acknowledged dish, which is not the same thing as every known dish. Look up sole (and very properly they only recognise Dover sole ... it is high time a law was brought in forbidding the lesser varieties such as Lemon and Southwold from sharing that great name) and there are something like 148 different ways of cooking or garnishing the filleted fish. Veronique – white wine sauce with halved white grapes, glazed; that is the extent of it. If you wanted to try a little *nouvelle cuisine* – say garnish fillets of Dover sole with slivers of coconut and kiwi fruit and pine kernels soaked in raspberry vinegar – it might be delicious but it is not a *recognised* dish, so it doesn't count. It is of course a Good Thing that we have moved away from such rigidity, but I am not sure that there was not some sort of security for the customer in the old days, when no-one in high class restaurants had vastly different food from other people in similar establishments around Europe.

There is a definite relationship between the cost of the ingredients and the end product price. I once did brilliantly in Stockholm when I ordered herring (£8.50 instead of £7.75 for the smoked salmon my host ordered) and got some smoked, some soused, some pickled, some raw fillets with cream, some rollmops. 'How did you know?' asked my host. 'The price,' said I. Herring is cheap, salmon expensive. If they charge a lot for herring there will be a good reason.

A restaurateur sets about the pricing like this: he decides what is to be the average 'spend' per customer, and aims to break even if he is 60% full for each meal. He then puts together prices that will make it hard for his customers to eat for much less than the average spend he has in mind. Thus there will be

a minimum charge for each first course. If soups are priced between £2.50 and £4 the first £2 is charged in order not to let
you get away with paying less; the rest reflects the value of the
dish.

Look at menus with care although they were probably not
written with any. Charging extra for vegetables is one rotten
trick: get your own back and embarrass the *maître d'* by asking
whether the tartar sauce is included in the price of the scampi.
Cover charges are iniquitous though if prices are moderate it is
reasonable to charge for bread and butter.

Restaurants hate serving bread and butter, especially in quantity – which is why waiters are trained to remove the bread
basket as quickly as they can without irritating the customer.
The more bread and butter people eat, the less likely they are
to order puddings, and the profit on puddings is substantial. If
you like bread, don't be put off, go ahead and order more. If
you like it hot, ask for it hot. Amazingly, nine out of ten waiters
will take the whole bread basket away when you ask for warm
bread, as though there is no other bread in the place. If the
butter comes in a paper-wrapped packet, cross out the service
charge.

The reason that restaurants change the menu has nothing to do
with the well-being of their customers. In fact it is the reverse –
most customers go to a particular place to eat a particular dish
and are furious when they discover that the dish they came to
eat is not being served that day. This is why steak houses,
burger parlours and sushi bars do so consistently well. You
know what you are going for, and it is always available.

The reason you can't get chicken in tamarind sauce in a restaurant this week when it was so delicious last time is that the
chef was bored with it and wanted to cook something else.

It is as simple as that. Ask a man of genius to do the same
thing day after day and he turns into a pack horse. There was a
time, and it may sometimes still be the case, when people went

to the same restaurant day after day and came out groaning, 'Not grilled chicken and pineapple *again*' but on the whole folk go to a place because they have a particular dish in mind. A place that changes its menu every day, or week, or fortnight, does it to keep the staff interested in their work.

There are inevitably also places – like one at Woodbridge near my home in Suffolk – where the menu is treated as a holy text, not to be meddled with. They have sausage beans and chips, eggs bacon and chips, bacon tomato and chips but if you order sausage bacon and tomato they say No. Sorry. We Don't Serve That.

Analysis of a meal

It must be the ambition of every self-respecting customer to extract a better deal from the restaurant he chooses to patronise than that restaurant intends to give him. This needs careful, and organised, planning. As they say in the army, Time Spent in Reconnaissance is Seldom Wasted.

There are countries where the customer distributes hundred dollar bills to all staff in sight on the way to his table. This is a crude, but guaranteed, way to earn respect. It is also expensive. It is more important to create the impression that here is a man who will distribute largesse – if he is looked after properly – without putting it up front ... because there is no machinery for getting the tip money back if you are disappointed.

You book a table – ideally through someone who is prepared to sound like a high-powered secretary. You arrive at the restaurant and the waiter says, 'Have you booked?' You mumble and walk in, heading for a table laid for roughly the number in your party, and say, 'May we sit here?'

The odds are 7–4 against the waiter genially saying, 'Yes, of course'; odds-on that he will say, 'I'm sorry, that table is booked.' You then pretend to remember and say, 'Oh, yes, I have booked, name of Blenkinsop.' The truth is that much as restaurants like to pretend certain people have booked certain tables, it is nearly always untrue. If someone goes to a particular restaurant often, he will have his preferred table, but he will also be fond enough of the restaurant to sit anywhere.

Nice restaurateurs will ask you where you would like to sit rather than telling you where. If they direct you to a Siberia of a table, don't sit down; once seated you have to ask to move. Until your bottom is on the seat you are not a customer and they know that you could still leave without much fuss. *Bluff*. If you are told that the table you like the look of is booked, agree and tell them it was you who placed the booking. The longer you are standing up near a table, the more uncomfortable a waiter feels and the more likely you are to get your way.

To be fair to the restaurateur, it is very helpful for the staff to know how many people are going to turn up and roughly when they are expected. However brilliant a kitchen, there are two things it cannot do: a) cope with everyone coming in and wanting to order – and be served – at the same time; and b) generate real skill if there is no momentum.

When there is only one couple in a restaurant that is geared to serving twenty, lethargy rules: the cooks cannot cook and the waiters cannot wait. Only the man who washes the dishes will be pleased, and it is a poor ambition to want to be voted Man-of-the-Year by the dishwasher.

While restaurants like people to book, they also prefer a bird in the hand to one on the end of a telephone who said he would come. Lots of people who book don't turn up, only the

well-brought up cancel. When the restaurant that fancies itself asks a customer to reconfirm the booking on the morning of the day, or asks for a number where they can contact him, they do not seem to realise that the customer who won't turn up is the one who gives a false name and telephone number, and uses the confirmed booking as an option in the evening's entertainment. So if you turn up at a restaurant where you tried to get a reservation and were told that it was fully booked, it is surprising how often you get lucky – though they will go out of their way to convince you how extremely fortunate you are to get accommodated . . .

In 1957 I opened an Espresso coffee bar with Robert Morley. I did the work; he came in from time to time and sat at the window table so people passing saw him and the place flourished. Sadly for restaurateurs, the celebrities they would like their punters to see usually prefer to sit at the back, facing the wall, while customers they are more ashamed of insist on tables where they can watch (and occasionally join in with) the action.

If you are a pretty unimposing, ordinary sort of customer in respect of whom no head waiter is going to spruce himself up and shine his shoes before approaching you, let alone offer you a glass of wine while you decide what to order, it may be a good idea to telephone the restaurant in advance and leave an important sounding message for yourself. 'When Mr Johnstone arrives . . . he has booked a table for three at 8.30 . . . please ask him to ring the Minister's Private Office immediately. He knows the number.' This sort of gamesmanship will certainly help you to be treated with respect – even if it is tinged with downright disbelief.

OK. You are sitting at the table of your choice, in the restaurant at which you have or meant to have booked a table. The next thing to do is to impress the waiter to ensure the very best service.

Waiters' steady suspicion is that the customer may be no

more important than they are themselves. Their worst fear is that the customer is an off-duty waiter from a rival establishment, there to give them a hard time, for a waiter who has been persistently polite to all-comers for a week has a desperate need to vent his bottled-up beastliness on someone else. A working waiter is suspicious of a punter with expertise. Someone who says 'Filet Sole Walewska, let me see that would be a fillet of Dover sole lightly poached in a *court bouillon*, garnished with shrimps and lobster and heavy cream' is likely to be a chef rather than a gourmet who will leave a hefty tip and be fun to serve.

What really impresses waiters is eccentricity. That and ordering things which are different and memorable. A waiter will remember you for what you eat, not what you are. 'There's the avocado and prawn cocktail lady,' he will say, or 'Here comes the thick toast man.'

Waiters are impressed by command. 'Take away the bread plate' is good, as is 'Remove the ashtray.' The more peculiar the demand the more impressed is the waiter, the better fun you will all have. 'I would like *two* napkins' will cheer up a waiter no end because it is different, or 'Could you please find me a pillow to put into the small of my back – I've come from my osteopath.' 'Please do not tell callers I am here' makes you sound important, so does shuffling a great wad of notes and asking the waiter the distance to the nearest betting shop that you can reach in time for the 2.45 at Sandown Park.

Another tack is ostentatious wastefulness. Ask for a very dry Martini, straight up with an olive . . . then eat the olive, say 'Delicious' and ask the man to remove the drink. This behaviour is so totally out with a waiter's experience that he will immediately realise you are someone very special (speciality is assessed by how different you are from the average client). Special people get special service. 'Hey chef, a fillet steak . . . for the man who left the martini and ate the olive.' The odds are the meat will be cut generously from the thick end with all gristle removed, for no one wants to lose a good customer like that.

Right. Now you are sitting at the table of your choice, in the restaurant you have selected and it is established that you are 'special'. Next the waiter brings you the menu.

It would be social suicide to ask him what he suggests: a) because that is what everyone else does and b) because the chef has told the waiter to push the navarin of lamb and there must be some good reason for that request which will not have a lot to do with it being absolutely delicious.

Put yourself in the waiter's position. Someone he has never seen before comes in and says what do you recommend? Well, you recommend whatever is going off so that you, the waiter, don't have to eat it for dinner. Or you recommend the most expensive thing on the menu because 15% of smoked salmon is worth more than 15% of tomato soup. If the customer asks whether the fish is fresh does he really think you are going to say, 'No, it last saw the sea a fortnight ago'? Everything is equally delicious as far as the waiter is concerned, to tell you so is his job. If you really want him to tell you what to eat try 'What do you suggest I eat that will put me in the mood to give you a huge tip when I have finished dinner?'

In most restaurants there are dishes which are not listed on the menu . . . like a couple of partridges or a red mullet . . . but you must wait to be offered off-menu food; Joseph Wechsberg wrote, after visiting Charles Gundel's Budapest restaurant, 'My friends had warned me expressly against ordering dishes that were listed on the menu. If you want to be respected, ask for something that's not on the bill of fare.'

Don't be ashamed to look at other people's plates as they are carried past you. I quite often ask other customers if they like what they are eating. At worst they can say nothing, but usually they'll tell me – especially if it isn't very good. Be careful which people you ask. Well brought-up Englishmen will say it's all right when it's foul and very nice when it's OK. Take the advice of foreigners or badly brought-up diners.

Order what you would like to eat, even if it slightly different

from the menu description. If you want the dish without butter or with extra sauce, tell the waiter. Again, it will make you special. The cook will be more interested in 'one Guinea fowl with rosemary, easy on the butter' than in 'one guinea fowl du jour'; more interest usually means better food.

Some restaurants have puddings which take a long time to prepare and if you plan to end your meal with a fruit soufflé or an apple dumpling, it is a good idea to examine the bottom half of the menu, or ask to see the pudding menu, before you make up your mind about the main course. You should plan a meal. If there is no dessert that takes your fancy, you must order accordingly. If there are two puddings you want, it should make a difference to what you decide to eat first.

Good restaurants give their customers something to keep them amused while they wait for the first course: a miniature puff pastry case with shrimp, aubergines or quail's egg. Some crudités, or an anchovy straw. Foolish restaurants give you bread and butter so that you stuff yourself and don't eat pudding.

If you are sensible you should gauge roughly how long your first course will take in getting to you and order something instant – like a portion of vegetable terrine between two of you – while they bake your snails or stuff your bespoke ravioli with a purée of wild mushrooms.

Finally there is the vexed question of tipping. In *A Farewell to Arms*, Hemingway writes about going to a restaurant and with his enviable economy of words ends the chapter 'We did not leave a tip. We were not going to go there again.'

There are a number of reasons for leaving a tip and certainly the way you will be received next time is an important one. Tipping is an evil, but if you have been to a country where there is no tipping, you may agree that it is a necessary evil. In countries behind the Iron Curtain, where you don't tip, you don't get what you or I would call service, either. You order. You sit. You wait. When you are served you find there is no fork or no salt – and no one is interested.

The very best system is for service to be included in the price of the meal. Ideally this percentage goes to the staff who serve you (although it seldom does) and you are expected, if the service was especially caring, to leave a little loose change as a sign of appreciation. $12\frac{1}{2}\%$ for service is fair, make this up to 15% if you were very pleased and make it up in cash if you are paying by credit card, as the gratuities signed away on plastic find their way to the intended beneficiary only with difficulty. In the United States service is not generally included in the bill and waiters are taxed at a notional 7% of the bills they make out. The 7% is because waiters managed to convince the Internal Revenue that there were among their clients some swine who didn't leave them anything at all. Had I been the tax man I doubt I would have believed this, for if you tip less than 10% the waiters take you by the throat, gently explaining as they shake you that you are taking money out of their pockets, food from their children's mouths, and should be locked up. Brave men then take back the 8% they had offered for indifferent service, but there are not too many brave men around to tell the tale.

It is important to remember that the good service which deserves tips has nothing to do with the quality of the meal – although a good waiter would be a fool to take a job in a restaurant where the food is poor. Good service means that the food arrives at your table at the right temperature. That you are served not instantly – that is not the waiter's responsibility – but at least before the people at the next table who ordered the same dish after you. Your plate should be removed as soon as everyone at your table has emptied their plates or pushed the knife and fork together if they are British, started smoking if they are Portuguese. If you finish the bread more should be available. The same goes for butter, iced water, coffee. If you drop your cutlery, clean cutlery should be brought. If you eat messy food, they should bring a clean napkin. The bill must come soon after you ask for it – but not before unless it is 2.30 a.m. and everyone else left hours before.

If the bill is much less than you expected, it may be because the waiter has left something off the bill in order that you will be pleased and surprised, and leave him an extra large tip. I once came across this on British Rail. After three courses and wine and brandy I asked for the bill, which came to £3.75. I said to the steward (as I believe they like to be called), 'My bill should be more than this.' He winked at me, and like a pompous prat I said it again. He kept on winking. If you accept the wink and pay the bill, leaving an extravagant tip on the grounds that you expected a bigger bill and the extra money might as well go to the waiter as the restaurant, you are an accessory to a crime. If a waiter wants to steal from his employer let him take money out of the till – like a proper thief.

The Trolley Syndrome

The history of the restaurant trolley has not been as faithfully recorded as, say, the history of the cinema ... but it first played a large part some time towards the end of the nineteenth century. Huge trolleys, their silver hoods covering the meat or fish that was laid on a tray over a jacket of boiling water heated by spirit lamps, were trundled around the grill-rooms of the civilised world on metal wheels. White-hatted chefs carved from the legs and saddles and sirloins, and in my youth they expected to be tipped 2d for their skill. 2d is no longer adequate but tipping the man who carves your meat remains one of the most cost-effective gratuities. Tip him – or let him know you will tip by fiddling with your wallet, then tell him how you particularly like the knuckle, or crispy pieces, or crackling, and your plate will be put in front of you full of what you would have served yourself had no-one been watching.

In the orderly days between the wars restaurants would advertise the day of the week on which saddle of lamb, boiled mutton and caper sauce, baked ham or sirloin of beef was to be served. Poached salmon hogged the Friday trolley with little concern for which was the established church of the land.

There was a sensible reason for having trolleys then, because hotel architects, who never thought to consider that the close juxtaposition of kitchen and dining room might be a Good Thing, usually put kitchens into basements. Boys earning 10/- a week then ran up and down the stairs with the food, which got cooler and less desirable *en route*. It also diminished in quantity, for boys had tasting spoons in their pockets and were hungry. *Hors d'oeuvre* trolleys were first sighted some two decades after the main dish trolleys. Twenty or more dishes rotated in front of the confused diner, offering him any combination of their varied delights.

And now there are sweet and cheese trolleys too, presumably designed more for the convenience of the server than the delectation of the customer. Cheese and puddings are both more likely to come at the right temperature via the pastry or larder chef of the old days than from an *in situ* collection. Some restaurants have refrigerated trolleys for sorbets, which are admirable from the point of view of man's achievement, but take up a lot of space and it is as uncomfortable to be run over by these as by any other vehicle in the armoury of the frustrated chefs who steer them.

My advice is, stick to the meat trolley. Make sure that you like what is on offer on the pudding trolley, that it has been assembled for the customers' delectation rather than the facility of the staff. There should be dishes of the stuff, rather than mean-looking individual trifles and mousses and crème caramels.

This is probably a good place to discuss cheese boards, as

opposed to cheese trolleys. Cheese boards are more common than trolleys, though both are money-losers for the restaurateur. The establishment has to show more cheeses than it will ever sell, and must keep each one looking beautiful, which means paring away at the outside at regular intervals. Also, people order whatever looks best, so the less good-looking pieces, even when they are excellent, steadily deteriorate and finish up in the sauce that covers the staff fish.

Waiters have an infuriating habit of cutting minute servings of cheese, because when you ask for cheddar they do not know whether you are going to add, 'Oh and some stilton – and a piece of camembert – and I'd like to try the chèvre.' If you say, 'I would like a lot of Double Gloucester' he knows where he stands; then if he gives you too little, ask for more.

Unless the choice of biscuits looks particularly appetising, ask for bread or rolls and say if you like them hot. You are paying the bill.

Garnishes

In the old days garnish for meat – steak, chops, escalope, roast chicken, pretty well anything really – was a lettuce leaf, a sprig of watercress, a wedge of lemon, half a grilled tomato and a large mushroom cap that had been 'turned' (ribbed) and kept in lemon water so that its colour was preserved. The fact that these things were all pretty disgusting and no one ate them was as nothing to the benefit of being able to decant a small amount of meat on to a large plate without leaving any gaps: that is what garnishes are about — making mean portions appear generous.

They are also about making boring things look interesting — so a dish of boiled new potatoes is 'garnished' with chopped parsley or fresh green mint leaves.

In classic French cuisine, virtually every dish has its authorised garnish: green pea soup gets *croûtons* (small cubes of stale bread fried in bacon fat); clear soups are given smooth ovals of forcemeat that reflect the flavour of the broth; vegetable soups of the minestrone family have cheese strewn over the top of each serving; turtle soup has sherry. Why? Because it says so in the book and no one bothered to think about it. Until *nouvelle cuisine* came along.

Nowadays garnishes are left very much to the chef's discretion . . . and he might use fresh flowers or kiwi fruit, or both.

Garnishes should complement the taste and add to the beauty of a dish. So if you are given a hollowed out tomato stuffed with minced mushrooms and breadcrumbs, the cook has missed the point and produced an extra vegetable rather than a garnish.

Some garnishes have much appeal, not infrequently more appeal than the dish they accompany. I have left *escalopes viennoise* and eaten the sieved hard-boiled egg, anchovy fillets, capers and slice of lemon that adorned it. And the garnish that comes with a roast pheasant — gravy, bread sauce and toasted buttered breadcrumbs — is a meal in itself and has to be when the pheasant is old and tough or over the top — hung for so long that the innards taint rather than the flesh is flavoured.

A customer has no 'divine right' to a garnish in a restaurant. Cheese over a dish that demands cheese, lemon over anything you fancy is par for the course and should not be denied you; that about exhausts your rights.

Watch garnishes and try to work out why they are there: to enhance the dish or for some ulterior motive: sprigs of parsley more often than not hide a punctured chicken's breast, a blemished potato or split fillet of fish.

Wine

This is not a book about wine. It is a book about restaurants. People wishing to learn about wine have a substantial bibliography, growing more substantial by the day, within easy reach. Masters of Wine, once an endangered species, the very rarest of birds, now swoop down on wine regions regularly and fill the food and drink pages of papers and magazines with their words of wisdom.

And the danger of this, it seems to me, is that it encourages people to drink better wines than they can appreciate, making them spend more money on old wines with complicated lineages long before they can even identify the rudimentary clues: the American oak, the fruit, the tannin, the spice. Magazines publish wines of the week, buys of the month, wines which in the eyes of the tasting panel are of outstanding value. These are only really useful if you want to serve wine to someone who knows more about it than you do: you will feel safe if you can produce a New Zealand Chardonnay and announce, 'Oz Clarke said that this was the best on the wine and food programme.' Sensible people will buy cheaper wines from their local supermarket and taste one against the other before deciding whether the price difference is justified by the difference in quality. Then, armed with a few ideas about what they like and can roughly afford, they will know more or less what to look for on a restaurant wine list.

There are rules about wine, but they are neither hard nor fast. If you are eating a juicy underdone rump steak, it is generally considered that the accompanying drink should be a full red wine; a delicate white wine is the one least likely to overwhelm the flavour of a steamed fish and no dish should be overwhelmed; an iced dessert wine, deep yellow with sweetness, is the best to order with your soft fruit yet it is also drunk by connoisseurs with *pâté de foie gras*. Suggestions as to what to drink with what are based simply on good sense: a subtle flavour will be overwhelmed by rich cheese, and red wine with oysters actually sets up a slight chemical reaction. But don't be bullied. Remember that these are only guidelines and if you happen to like a rich fruity hock with lamb cutlets, then ask for it. Wine buffs write and talk as though the food and wine will be in your mouth at the same time, that one is there to be poured over the other. This is bullshit. Gustatory enjoyment comes from food and wine and cigars of your liking. So far no one has said that a Monte Cristo is the only cigar to smoke after Armagnac, Romeo and Juliet after Calvados ... but the time may yet come.

Let me explain about wine and restaurants. Restaurants need the expenditure on drink; without it they would have to charge more for food. (In Israel, where few drink wine, the food is more expensive than anywhere else in the world – and is not that good, either.) The management reckons to 'earn' at least £2 a head in profit on wine, the serving of which involves one old boy pulling a cork. As a result of this they can hire several other old boys to make a soup which involves real work: buying half a dozen ingredients and using skill and gas and cream and saucepans and silver and plates. The price of wine is therefore not cost price plus 200% but cost price plus £6, which is what they need by way of profit per bottle. If it is a very expensive bottle, they might add a little more for luck. It is perfectly acceptable for a wine bought cheaply a few years ago to appear on a wine list at £20 by virtue of its scarcity and maturity.

If you want to gain an insight into the pricing structure of a restaurant's wine list, look at the non-vintage champagne. Lanson, Mumm, Mercier, Pommery, Clicquot, Heidsieck Dry Monopole, Goulet – none of these would wholesale at more than £9 a bottle. If less than £20 is charged for some, that is good news. When the cheapest champagne whose name is familiar costs well over £20 you are in an expensive place and are probably safest with the house wine ... or the house champagne.

Naturally the restaurateur wants you to drink lots of wine, which means a big bill which means (or should mean) a big tip. But it is *your decision*. If you like beer, go ahead and order it. In ethnic restaurants beer or cider is often a great deal more appropriate to the food on offer than is expensive wine.

The clue is *not* to buy wine better than you can appreciate and *not* to order good wine to impress the staff. They won't be impressed, they will see through you and giggle at you from the kitchen. Of course they will want to sell you the more expensive stuff, though they realise that if you are not pleased with their advice the tips will shrink. If you really don't know what to drink, ask the wine butler what he would suggest that costs under £12 a bottle that would go with what you are eating.

If the wine waiter lets you taste the wine before he pours it and you *really* don't like it, it may be corked, although in my many years of tippling I have only come across a very few examples of this. But if it is *not* what the man said it would be – i.e. sweet, or 'velvety' – and you take a second sip and it is no better, send it back.

A few easy tips: Spanish Riojas are almost consistently all right; exported Australian, New Zealand and Californian wines never fall below an acceptable quality level and are often excellent; white German wines are seldom very dry and can be delicious and Alsatian wines (which with few exceptions are dry) are not very expensive and taste of sunshine and fruit. If you are faced with a large wine list and are feeling rich (and confused), champagne is a good choice, and can decently be drunk with virtually any food – although if you are having something stew-like with garlic, a bottle of house red would make more sense. Or maybe two bottles.

With Our Compliments, Sir

There is no such thing as 'free' food, and one of the more rotten customs that has grown up is the proffering of food or drink 'with the compliments of the management'. You sit down and along comes a simpering waiter, bearing a glass of indifferent wine or a few snippets of food and murmuring, 'This is on the house.' What they mean is that with the prices you are about to pay they can afford to throw in 50p worth of something under no specific heading on your bill — designed to impress and make simpletons feel they are getting a special deal. Noticeably they give you what they want to get rid of, rather than what you actually want.

If *someone wants to offer me something for nothing let it be what I have ordered* — or give me a discount off my bill. If they want to give me brandy, let it be offered when I am considering a liqueur, not after I have refused it.

If you are really brave:

Waiter: These canapés are with our compliments.
Customer: Oh, good. I was going to order dinner but now I'll just have these.

Complaining

There are people who think that if they go to a restaurant and get something bad, they only have to point it out to the waiter

and he will replace it with something good. In fact bad restaurants serve bad food and if you complain about the bad chicken, you will be brought bad duck. It is all right to complain if something is at the wrong temperature, like cool soup (although you tend to get coolish soup in France and no one makes a fuss) or if you have expressly asked for meat to be cooked in one way – say rare lamb cutlets – and they arrive cooked differently – well done.

'Please would you make this soup hotter' is fair; if the waiter thinks it was quite hot enough when he brought it, and if it was your telling of the story about the chef in Vienne standing you an 1897 Armagnac that caused it to get cold, he is quite likely (and would feel himself entitled to) revenge himself on you.

If properly trained, he will put the soup plate under the grill so that the rims become white hot, bring it back and put it just off centre in front of you, hoping like hell that you will straighten the plate and burn your fingers, affording him the chance to say, 'Hot enough now, is it, sir?'

Let me remind readers that it is only worth complaining to the optimum capability of the establishment in which you are eating. 'The omelette Arnold Bennett was much better at the Savoy' is an unjustifiable complaint at the Café Royal, for example; complaint is only worth the effort and the subsequent disruption if there is a 90% chance that it will result in improvement.

Restaurant staff believe customers can be divided into two sorts: those who complain and those who don't. (In fact pretty well any one blows up if driven to the utmost edge of his tolerance.) It is true to say, though, that the English complain least of all western nations, which is probably something to do with their upbringing, back to the nannied childhoods of Don't Make a Fuss, Good little Boys and Girls Leave their Plates Clean, Think of all the Children Dying in Africa. Thirty years on, most Englishmen would do anything rather than make an issue about over-salted soup, doubtful fish or burnt rice pudding . . . *Lovely rice pudding for dinner again* is more about familiarity than quality.

Rather as it is silly to lose the no claim bonus on your car insurance for an insignificant claim, so should you not complain unless something major has gone wrong: then, provided you have the justification you must attack with passion. Complaining is not something you can practise against an emergency. Wait for the right occasion.

I was in Melbourne once, sitting in the garden of a restaurant whose speciality was Queensland mud crab. They cooked the crabs in wire baskets suspended in boiling water and every fifteen minutes or so a man would run from the kitchen and decant a dozen grizzly-looking crabs on to the plates of the next twelve customers who had ordered the beasts. Then he would disappear. For some reason (and this is something which happens to food writers more than to other people) my mud crab had escaped the pot and was raw: dead and on the warm side by virtue of having been in close proximity to crabs that had been boiled; nevertheless raw. I waited fifteen minutes until the waiter came out with his next batch of crustaceans and as he passed my table I quietly said, 'My crab is raw', sociably — as one chap might speak to another. He walked past. I said it more loudly and at last he came up and said, 'Whassamatter?' 'This,' I said, still friendly. 'This crab is raw . . . look,' and I showed him the flesh which should have been white and aromatic but was a glutinous grey. He looked at it suspiciously, as though it were my fault and then he said, *'No-one else has complained.'*

It was a good remark. It was true, it made me feel a shit and it implied that all the other customers in the garden deserved a pat on the back.

I always liked the story of Tallulah Bankhead (though I have heard the same story in respect of other legendary American ladies who shunned teetotalism) who went to a party, drank a great deal of liquor and on the way home found a seal, which she brought back to her house and put in the bath. The next day she awoke with a sore head and rang for the housekeeper to bring her coffee. She went on ringing – in vain. When she finally dragged herself downstairs she found a note on the kitchen table from her late employee: 'Dear Miss Bankhead. I have left. I have left because of the seal. I don't like seals. I would have mentioned this before but didn't think it would come up.'

'I didn't think it would come up' is a phrase dear to us all, especially when we are contemplating a complaint. I once booked a table at a London restaurant. Would I like to eat in the dining room or the garden? It was a fine June evening and I said garden. A huge black cat sat on my table – and I don't like cats. Should I have told them when I booked 'I don't like cats, am also very unfond of anyone wearing Dr Scholl sandals (feeling that if people have things wrong with their feet it should be a private matter between them and what is at the end of their legs); come to that I loathe being served by waiters reeking of tobacco or waitresses stinking of scent, people wetting their fingers and describing circles on the rims of their wine glass to bring forth a high-pitched shriek . . .'; if I really get down to it the list of things I don't care for, that particularly work towards the disenjoyment of my meal, is too long to enumerate even in a book, in which one is encouraged to go on a bit.

When things 'come up' it is as well to write off the occasion and start again. I have found, over the years I worked in the restaurant trade, that once things go wrong – even slightly wrong such as a cat on the table, cockroach in soup, a leg breaking from a chair or a waiter dressing the crab with custard instead of mayonnaise, things continue to go wrong. From the point of view of the caterer he might as well cut his losses. When a customer said to me, 'See here, the soup isn't hot enough,' I would say, 'Get out.'

It made sense in the long run – because once a punter starts to moan everyone round him thinks maybe he has a point and moans in empathy. Bounce out the odd innocent and a huge number of potentially guilty get the message and behave properly.

But this book is to advise you the customer, not them the caterers.

So, if you are sure that your complaint is justified, and you have exhausted the primary route to gratification – telling the waiter – you must then resort to the only other accepted way of showing disapproval of a restaurant: refusing payment. If you are brave – and big – tell the staff you won't pay and ask them to call the police. They might take you at your word, but the police can do nothing more than ask for your name and address.

The thinking of the establishment will be that as you are obviously not going to come back they might as well get some money out of you on this, your only visit. They also know that no-one in their right mind likes a scene nor wants one to occur in front of their guests at what was presumably supposed to be a convivial occasion. So I reluctantly advise that *if* justice is on your side and the management continues pigheaded, pay by cheque or credit card, cancel the payment, send a cheque for what you think they should have charged and invite them to sue you in court.

We do have laws that protect the consumer – but none that can successfully be used to get gastro-justice. I have been served lemon sole when the menu promised Dover. The difference in price is significant, in quality substantial – not only in the taste but in the texture. Dover sole, the caterer's dream fish, has flesh that remains firm even if it's overcooked: overcooked lemon sole tastes like blotting paper, falls to bits on the fork and to my mind is a boring fish unless very fresh and served only with lemon and butter. Confronted with this cheap dull fish masquerading as a pricey delicacy, my only legal resource would be to ring the local council and ask the Trading Standards Officer to hurry on over before my plate was cleared away . . . and I can't help but wonder how many Trading Standards Officers would know the difference.

We restaurateurs, discussing the problems of difficult customers, have concluded that it is the nature of our business that attracts troublemakers. In life you need to go through the laborious business of computer-dating, courtship and marriage (or the expense of advertising, interview and job specification) before you have any right to shout at someone who has failed to please. In a restaurant you can scream at people for the price of a cup of coffee, insult a waiter for suggesting that you sit at this — rather than that — table and then leave. There are people who use restaurants as places in which to vent their anger. I mention this simply to give a reason for the occasional haughtiness of serving staff — the axiom 'the customer is always right' was dreamt up by a customer who was almost certainly wrong. Sadly, there are waiters who believe that attack is the best form of defence; they too are wrong.

From the caterer's point of view, throwing out a customer is the very last resort: it leads to noise, disruption, financial loss (you can't evict *and* charge), upsets other clients and gains for you a reputation as an intolerant innkeeper, which is quite hard to sustain in the long run ... I mean once they come to hear of it, people always expect you to throw out at least one customer per meal. I mention this simply to inform putative troublemakers that there is small likelihood of being evicted from eating houses for anything less serious than assault or throwing up over someone they rate highly.

Cooking at Table 1: Food You Can Read By

There was a restaurant on Ibiza where the house speciality was a soufflé surprise, a block of ice cream covered by hot sweet meringue strewn with sugar that had begun to caramelise. Each time it was served the house lights were dipped and a waiter brought the confection, bedecked with a sparkler. The 'surprise' lasted twenty seconds, cheered up the punters and made everyone aware that here was an excellent pudding that was fun.

When I wrote about atmosphere I stressed that the enjoyment of the customer is more important than the feeding of the caterer's ego. Whether it is a Good Thing to have a man appear with a mobile stove and cook *at* you while you are dining is entirely a matter of taste. In Pembroke there is a place where *every* dish is cooked for you at your table. This is fine if you have gone to a restaurant in order to be entertained by a frustrated chef. The main trouble is that a restaurant where the staff is cooking pancakes and fillet steaks at you cannot be a place where the meal is the background to conviviality and good conversation. A frying pan in flames, even three tables away from yours, is an appalling conversation stopper — quite apart from being a considerable fire hazard. I am sad to say that there are as yet no recorded disasters started by a *Crêpe Suzette* or *Steak au Poivre Flambé*. A small dining room would need to burn down for the practise to be banned and cookery relegated to the kitchen — from where it should not have emerged.

One of the reasons for flambéd food is to preserve the myth that cooking is difficult . . . which is why the pancake cook fools around with five liqueurs, a whoosh of oil, a slice of butter and some brown sugar. If he confined himself to butter, sugar, lemon juice and Grand Marnier you might realise what a simple confection it is.

Another restaurant performance is Steak Tartare (which is not set alight unless the waiter is very unlucky). I rather liked it before I gave up eating red meat, but *I don't want to see it made*. It bores me to watch a man I do not know whisking oil into an egg in a depression in minced meat. The whole thing is no more than a means of extracting tips . . . because for each of the multiple ingredients — chopped onion, gherkin, parsley, shallot,

capers, anchovy, etc, etc, the waiter says, 'A little more or is this about right, sir?' and who can fail to overtip a man who has obeyed a dozen commands in the space of two minutes?

Bespoke cooking is not necessarily good cooking — rather the reverse. The time when you need a waiter with a stove is when the conversation between you and your guests has ground to a halt and you are too scared to cut your losses and leave.

Cooking at Table 2: Improving Bad Food

As a young man Lord Gowrie, the former Minister for the Arts, went to dine with his uncle, who watched the lad add salt and pepper to his food and said, 'Grey, cooking at table? We don't care for that a great deal.'

I do go in for cooking at table when necessary. Many years ago I went to a restaurant opening. The management had ingenuously invited a hundred people and given each a menu, telling them to order *à la carte*. I ordered fillet steak with a *béarnaise* sauce. After a while the waiter came back, saying he wished to apologise: the chef could not make *béarnaise* sauce because the copper pans lined with silver, essential to the preparation of a *béarnaise*, had not yet arrived. He was desolate . . . all that kind of thing.

I said I would eat the beef without the *béarnaise*, if I could have a raw egg. To the great shame of my wife I made the *béarnaise* myself, at table. I put the yolk in a wine glass, melted the butter from the butter dish in another, over the candle, dripped the ghee on to the egg and used the lemon, chilli, vinegar

and pepper that had come with oysters to lend piquancy, beating the mixture with a fork. This made enough noise to attract a sizeable audience to the table, which cheered and asked me to cook things to add to their food.

I am not proud of this episode (and my wife continues very ashamed) but I do hate waiters who invent dishonest excuses for their failings. The chef had too much to do to make a complicated sauce. I would have understood that.

I once asked for sweetbreads in a restaurant in Chelsea. The waiter came back after a while and said, 'The chef thinks the sweetbreads are not quite fresh enough to suit such a discriminating client as you.' I knew this meant he was out of sweetbreads. My guest bet me a fiver I was wrong — so I said I actually liked nothing more than not-very-fresh sweetbreads. The waiter went away, came back again and said that really the chef thought they were quite off. Good, I said, the offer the better. It took ten more minutes and two more journeys to the kitchen before the man admitted they were out of sweetbreads, and I won my bet.

If the salad dressing is foul, I ask for oil, vinegar, lemon and sugar and make my own. (Damn it, I won't be going back so I might as well enjoy myself while I am there.) Order sherry before your meal, leave a little in the glass and then you will have something with which to cheer up a second rate soup. Cream is always on the pudding trolley — and it is very enjoyable to see the dismay on the face of the trolley's driver when you lean over and pluck the cream jug from his passing cart to pour its contents over your spinach.

In the old days, Lyons Corner Houses charged 2d for 'cover' (bread and butter) and 3d for tea. It is said that the tramps who could afford a fivepenny spread used to sit down, drink their tea, then fill the cup with tomato ketchup, worcester sauce, salt, pepper and sugar (all free), top the mixture up with hot water and have tomato soup on the house. I doubt Heinz's good cream of tomato soup has many more ingredients than that.

Because customers steal peppermills (as well as teaspoons), restaurants have taken to buying mills so large they will not fit in bags or pockets – and need professionals to manipulate them. The lunacy of hiring a chef to create a dish, and then have a waiter rush up and offer to pour pepper all over it before it has even been tasted deserves a moment's thought. Their worry about you nicking the mills (coupled with their fear of making you feel pepperless) causes this dilemma. You might ask the waiter to leave the mill on the table, offering to pay a cash deposit on it, or, when the pepperpot is poised above your dish, ask whether the chef forgot to put pepper in the food. It will pull them up in their tracks, and distinguish you as someone who can be bullied only with forethought. That is no bad thing.

Women Hosts

Restaurants are based on deep rooted sexism (where do men go when they want a better meal than their wives can cook? To a place where a man is in charge of the food) and cannot cope with the notion that a woman should be hosting a party. I know a woman in America who after two children, a second degree, and three years at law school finally earned her first paycheck. She took her husband out to dinner for the first time in their fifteen years together. The fiendish waiter pricked the bubble by handing her husband the bill; she gave him *her* credit card, he returned and handed the slip to the husband to sign.

Women who want to host a party and avoid this kind of

irritation should ring up in advance and explain. 'I, Mrs Smith, am the host. I, Mrs Smith, am paying the bill ... do you understand? If you fail to treat me as the host you will receive no tip and I, Mrs Smith, the host, will refuse to pay the service charge.'

It is as simple as that. Money talks, but the promise of money withheld talks even more loudly.

Children in Restaurants

Of course it is foolish to generalise, but on the whole children (unless bred to it and trained from an early age) are bored by restaurant meals that involve long waits at unfamiliar tables. In Italy children are, from the point of view of accompanying adults, the passport to success. Everyone cries, 'Ah Bambino Bellino!' to anything under eight years old and feeds it with slices of honeybread, snippets of food and glasses of coke. Children in southern countries are particularly useful if you have failed to book a table, and I am surprised that no one has yet thought of renting out small children to casual restaurant-goers.

Children appreciate discipline which they do not get in places where, officially at least, the customer is boss. There are two kinds of parent: those who allow their children to roam about the dining room importuning other guests and they who keep snapping at them to sit still and behave. I honestly do not know which is worse, but I do think that children in restaurants are bad news unless they are asleep.

If you have to take a child out to lunch or dinner, order

something that will not take too long to cook, impress on the staff how troublesome the child might become if the service is not fast and immaculate (you could try and tell them that the child kicks up a terrible fuss if his dad is not offered a bottle of free champagne — after all you don't have a lot to lose, having started off the evening with a child in tow). The more difficult-to-open plastic envelopes of sugar and ketchup, mayonnaise and instant coffee you can find to distract the child, the more peaceful the meal will be.

Now and then you encounter a cloakroom attendant who will check in your child for the duration of the meal and humour it. This can work out cheaper than leaving it at home with a babysitter, but as a rule infants have to be non-mobile to be left among the hats and coats.

N.B. *Goujons* is restaurant-speak for fishfingers, *bitok* for a hamburger and *pommes frites* for chips. Waiters don't like bringing tomato ketchup to the table in case you take too much and deprive the staff of their share.

Food on the Move

For some ten years I ran the catering operation at Regents Park Open Air Theatre ... and I would like to think that the fact there was no alternative source of food or drink within ten minutes fast walk in any direction never affected my catering philosophy. I would like to think that.

From the consumer's point of view, it must be stressed that the harder it is to reach an alternative source of sustenance, the more you should respect what is on hand.

Especially does this apply to trains, boats and planes. On trains and boats my advice is to take your own ... a sharp knife, a freshly baked wholemeal loaf, some pre-sliced Scotch smoked salmon, a peppermill and a lemon ... which makes your fellow passengers jealous as hell even as you squirt lemon juice into their eye.

On aeroplanes it is clearly the ambition of the airlines to have you fly first class – and the last thing they want is for travellers in club or economy to arrive at their destination and say, 'That was a wonderful flight with terrific food, I shall never fly any other way.'

In economy the food is at best ordinary, in club satisfactory; it is the first class food which excels, some airlines actually seducing passengers on to their flights by the dishes on offer: there used to be a BA London-Boston-Detroit flight which people boarded at Boston expressly to get the wild salmon trout in anchovy butter and puff-pastry asparagus straws served in that two hour high-tea sector. It deserved a Michelin star denoting 'worth the detour'.

If you are flying less than first class (which makes sense as you save around £100 a flying hour, worth a bit of discomfort) tell them in advance that you are a vegetarian, Kosher, Chinese ... absolutely anything but that which is on offer to everyone else. Chinese is especially good value as they have the same Chinese dinner in club and economy. Again there is a sound argument for taking your own food – in sandwich form as there is unlikely to be room to prepare things. Buy the airline's orange juice and ask for much ice to be put into the glass ... and give it a sharpener from your duty free vodka.

British Rail serve excellent breakfasts and it is well worth tipping the steward before the meal with some word like 'I am really looking forward to my breakfast.' Someone is going to get the egg with the addled yolk; someone will be the last of the ten to be served from his tray: it is highly unlikely to be the person who crossed his palm with a £1 coin, especially if, when you pass him his gratuity, you ask his advice on where to sit. Since the buffets were taken over, there is not a lot of good advice I can give . . . other than to travel with a bottle of Escoffier Cumberland Sauce in your brief-case which improves the taste of just about everything they sell — except tea: tea-dust and milk-granules are soldered into the base of polystyrene containers to dissolve in God's good time if the water that is poured thereon is warm. Tea served in pots, at tables, in the afternoon is good. I treat long excursions on BR rather as I treat health farms, taking no food and lots of exercise . . . like walking up and down the carriages occasionally asking the buffet attendant to let me have a bottle of Perrier water.

Food Guides

I was recently engaged to write a book on the thirty best restaurants in Great Britain. The publishers decided to take those two and a half dozen that had received the greatest acclaim from the most recent Good Food, Ronay and Michelin guides. I started on this agreeable research and found that the first two restaurants on my list — one in Cambridge and the other in Bristol — had been sold and changed chefs within eight months of the guides' appearance. They will not feature in my book. The reason is that a talented caterer does not need to buy good will; he creates his own — buys an unsuccessful restaurant cheaply and makes a go of it.

When a place has a star, or a chef's hat, or a plaque stating that it is the Cambridge Restaurant of the Year, it is the team of owner, chef and waiter which has won the accolade. A new team needs re-assessment.

Although there are too many food guides, they are important in that they keep restaurateurs on their toes and provide for them a steady stream of customers. It should be borne in mind that owners and staff of restaurants, even when they do not change, have days off, have off days, sometimes recognise an inspector and make a special effort to achieve a rave review. The prices, the style of cooking and quality of the wine lists, the speciality which may still be on the menu (and will be if enough people have read the guide book and asked for it) are all important items in guides, as is their objective information: when they close, where they are, how much the *table d'hôte* costs . . . Which is why professionals prefer the red Michelin rather than the subjective Egon Ronay and Good Food Guides which deal with minutiae ('over sauced saddle of hare; dull vegetables').

What is true is that no guide book is wholly bad and the ones printed annually are infinitely better than the occasional ones that display no date. Remember that June would be the very last date for correcting copy for guide books published in November, bearing the date of the following year, and a great deal can happen in a few months. If you do go somewhere because it is recommended in a guide, it would be wise when booking to ask whether so-and-so is still the owner, or does such-and-such remain chef – guides on the whole do give the names of these key characters.

Because of our legal system, guides leave out places they do not rate (whereas in France every single town figures). This is disappointing and depressing: too many towns do not appear at all, even though there must be a strong argument for disclosing which of the unrated restaurants was the most rateable: even to be able to read under 'FRAMLINGHURST' that the nearest rated eating house is at Cumber, six miles south west, would be a help.

It is a good idea to go to restaurants with a notebook which you leave open at the side of your plate and scribble in from time to time. It can do no harm, and with a bit of luck will make the management think that you are there for some other reason than that you are hungry.

Restaurants and the Law

This is only just worth a chapter, for if you have to involve the judiciary in order to get satisfaction it makes a nonsense of the whole concept of a good meal served by concerned staff in agreeable surroundings. You are already lost and it is already *too late*. But nevertheless, rather on the grounds that the American nuclear force is geared to react rather than strike, it is as well to have an idea of where you stand.

A restaurant is obliged to publish in a prominent place a priced menu of the fare on offer and the minimum charge payable. It must be visible from a place outside the restaurant so you do not have to go in and get embarrassed asking, and find out and get embarrassed going out, pretending you don't like Szechuan cooking that much anyway. But it has to be said that there are thousands of places that do not display menus and very few prosecutions, just as there aren't many prosecutions against people who smoke in non-smoking compartments of trains, considering how often that law is breached.

There are also laws about the standard of service, the proportion of food on the menu that has to be available, the degree of responsibility of a restaurant that loses your umbrella or mink and how long a customer may sit over his coffee before he is thrown out or locked in.

But the most interesting aspect of restaurant law is that which involves booking tables and not turning up or, from the other side of the fence, booking a table and arriving to find no table available.

In case law, the customer is the more likely to lose: Mr and Mrs Duncan booked a table for two by telephone for the following day. But when they arrived at the restaurant there was no table, and they were rudely told there wouldn't be one for the rest of the evening. They had no choice but to go home. Mr Duncan wrote to the restaurant to complain, but the letter was not answered. So he decided to sue under the small claims procedure for breach of contract. He claimed the money spent getting to and from the restaurant, and a sum to compensate for disappointment and distress. The court ruled that the restaurant had breached its contract, but did not award the Duncans any compensation. The restaurant had only to pay the Duncans' £10 court fee.

Some years ago I went to a restaurant in Oxford, having not only booked, but confirmed the reservation and given instructions as to which wine should be offered to the county's Chief Education Officer, were he to arrive before I did. As it happened we arrived together and the place was full. The staff admitted the fault was theirs and offered us a bottle of champagne on the house. We weren't in the mood, and there was nowhere to sit. A party left after about half an hour, mostly because they were embarrassed at our plight. I doubt there was cause for a law suit, for we could have waited for half an hour before our first course arrived, and that is perfectly legal. But if you book a table and don't turn up – which happens more and more often – the restaurant can sue you. Of course it is not the best PR for a place to be famed as 'those people who sue customers for not turning up' and does give the punter a slight disincentive to book in case he forgets to cancel or is run over, leaving his estate to face the action; nevertheless it can be, and is, done.

A party of twenty booked a table for a Christmas party at a country club. The club confirmed the booking. On the evening only ten of the party turned up, and they were two hours late. The staff at the country club refused to serve them and then sued the party for breach of contract, claiming the profit they would have made on the twenty meals. The country club won and was awarded £215.

Irritating for the party, but you can see the restaurant's point. The great and angry Nico Ladenis has campaigned for the death penalty for no-show customers for many years and has recently taken to asking for the credit card number of people reserving tables and if they do not appear, charging their accounts with what they might have spent if they had eaten. History does not relate whether this deterrent works. Mr Worrall Thompson of Beauchamp Place has another good system: he takes bookers' telephone numbers and if they don't turn up he waits until the place closes, say at two in the morning, then rings the customer and asks whether he should let the staff go home now or should they carry on waiting.

There is no law about the quality of food served, so long as it does no irreparable harm.

I once went to a restaurant in Auckland, New Zealand, ordered a *contrefilet de boeuf béarnaise*, and was presented with a piece of beef so tenderised that it was like a hamburger, garnished with Crosse and Blackwell's salad cream. This, I suggested to the waiter who brought it, is not *contrefilet béarnaise*. 'How long have you been in New Zealand, sport?' was all he would say. I explained that the length of my stay was irrelevant to the duplicity of the menu but he walked away, muttering, 'Not long, I can tell.'

Technical Expressions

A random selection gleaned from overheard conversations in —
and menus of — the last dozen restaurants I visited.

Medium done: The chef is off and this is as good as you get

Rare: Food they have forgotten to cook

Well done: Waiter's reply to 'You have burnt my steak' — 'No,
it is well done.' Well done toast is what you smell in many
restaurants

Off: In respect of food — past it. In respect of people — gone.
Viz I'm off, which usually means I am going away, though it
can mean I'm past it

Stiff (verb): To leave without giving a tip

Runner: Someone who leaves without paying the bill

A chance customer: A non-resident in a hotel dining room

Gorilla: An untrained worker

Professional: Someone about to retire

Field Marshall: Carriage attendant or anyone else who wears
fancy uniform

A cover: A place setting. As in 'four covers on table 12'

Cover charge: A dubious device whereby the restaurant charges
you for sitting down

Florentine: With spinach

Espagnole: With tomatoes

Veronique: With grapes

Dubarry: With cauliflower

Meunière: Tossed in butter and lemon juice

Frite: Deep fried

Forestière: With mushrooms

Parsley: Green herb, principally used to hide blemishes and make stale food look appetising

St Germain: With dried peas

Mornay: With a cheese sauce, usually browned

Provençale: Contains garlic

Gibiers: Game

Volailles: Chicken, duck, turkey. Also squab

Quenelles: Forcemeat

Noisette: Literally nut. Used to describe fillet or tenderloin of meat

Farci: Stuffed

Au four: From the oven. A *pomme au four* is a baked potato

Sauté: Literally jumped. Food cooked in frying pan and tossed

En papillote: Cooked in an envelope of greaseproof paper or similar

Feuilleté: Cooked in puff pastry. Vol-au-vent in old-speak

Vacherin: A confection customarily built on meringue, nothing to do with *vache* – cow or *vacherie* – dirty trick.

Tiède: Lukewarm. A very trendy temperature at which to serve food

Assiette: Literally plate. *Assiette anglaise* – spam on a plate

Carré: Best end

Gratinée: Strewn with breadcrumbs and browned

Glazed: Finished off in heavily reduced stock usually with added sugar to achieve colour. Or browned under a grill for same effect

Marinated: Kept in a marinade

Marinade: A liquor to season and make tender the food you steep therein

Darne: A slice, as in *Darne de Saumon*

Ragout: A stew

Sorbet: A water ice (as opposed to ice cream)

Suprême: Breast. As in chicken – *suprême de volaille*

A la maison: The way we decide to serve it today

The Italian way: When the waiter tips the contents of his serving dish on to your plate

Wild: Not farmed. Wild salmon means something. Scotch salmon might just mean that the fish farm is north of Hadrian's Wall

Baby: Young or small

Mousse: Something that has been liquidised or passed through a sieve – often set with gelatine

Roulade: Rolled up – à la Swiss roll

Selle: Saddle; saddles of hare and rabbit tend to be called 'rable'

Boudin: Black pudding

Crêpe crepinette: Pancake, wrapped in a thin pancake

Salmis: Game stew

Estouffade: Pretentious French word for stuffing

Wine basket: Absurd contraption whereby bottles are presented at table in a prone position with a view to getting bigger tips by being seen to do pointless things. (It makes sense if you ordered the wine hours before the meal, and none when it has been brought from the cellar, uncorked and left for ten minutes)

Decant: Sensible thing to do to wines with a sediment, pointless otherwise

Finger bowl: Receptacle containing water in which to dip fingers after eating asparagus or feeling your dining companion

Tulip: A kind of glass

Pansy: A kind of waiter

Staff dinner: Anything you send back in disgust

Maître d's dinner: What you would like to have got

Hors d'oeuvre: Literally outside the main work. Actually French for starter

Plat du jour: Dish of the day. Should be ready and cooked especially for that meal

Entremet: Pudding course

Commis: A junior in the catering trade. Commis cook or commis waiter

Spelling mistakes on menu: Bear no relationship to the quality of the food – but tell you a bit about the expertise of the management

Menu gastronomique: Usually the best dishes they can put together

Menu surprise: Tends to be the most expensive things they can put together. Make sure the price is not also a surprise

Menu potager: Vegetarian menu

MP (on a menu): Market price. A thoroughly reprehensible practice that shames you into asking how much, or not ordering what you want, or entails sitting there worrying until you get the bill

SG: Depending on size, which is fair. Found in respect of very expensive dishes like lobster

A symphony of desserts: The chef is gay

Nouvelle cuisine: Small portions messed around by many hands usually served on large plates, food on top of sauce. Raspberry vinegar and kiwi fruit play their parts

Cuisine minceur: No-flour cooking, substances thickened with purée of vegetables or mushrooms. Caught on. Made author rich. Faded out